THE GUARDIAN

The Story of a Texas Ranger–Rough Rider, American Hero

K. D. Brogdon

iUniverse, Inc.
Bloomington

The Guardian
The Story of a Texas Ranger–Rough Rider, American Hero

This is a work of fiction. All of the characters, names, incidents, organizations, and dialogue in this novel are either the products of the author's imagination or are used fictitiously.

iUniverse books may be ordered through booksellers or by contacting:

iUniverse
1663 Liberty Drive
Bloomington, IN 47403
www.iuniverse.com
1-800-Authors (1-800-288-4677)

Because of the dynamic nature of the Internet, any Web addresses or links contained in this book may have changed since publication and may no longer be valid. The views expressed in this work are solely those of the author and do not necessarily reflect the views of the publisher, and the publisher hereby disclaims any responsibility for them.

Any people depicted in stock imagery provided by Thinkstock are models, and such images are being used for illustrative purposes only.

Certain stock imagery © Thinkstock.

ISBN: 978-1-4502-7945-1 (pbk)
ISBN: 978-1-4502-7946-8 (cloth)
ISBN: 978-1-4502-7947-5 (ebk)

Printed in the United States of America

iUniverse rev. date: 12/13/2010

Library of Congress Control Number: 2010917728

This book is dedicated to the Texas Rangers and to all of the men and women in law enforcement, especially those serving in the Tampa, Florida, police department, who protect us daily by placing their lives on that thin blue line. I have had the honor and privilege of walking in the footsteps of heroes for the past twenty-five-plus years. I have seen a fifty-two-year-old police corporal scale a chain-link fence and disarm a woman holding a nine-millimeter pistol before she could commit suicide. I have witnessed a police officer kick in the front door of a burning house and carry a ninety-year-old lady safely from her smoke-filled home. I have seen a young white police officer run up the exterior stairs of a burning building in order to carry a crippled seventy-two-year-old black male through the flames and then back down those stairs to safety. This was during the so-called race riots of the 1980s. I have seen great acts of heroism by men and women, none of them seeking or wanting any recognition for their acts. I have seen them cry as they have laid a friend, a partner, to rest.

I also send out a belated thanks to the men of the First United States Volunteer Cavalry Regiment, who answered a call to glory and helped to start a nation. For their dedication and commitment to children's charities, a special acknowledgment to the Tampa, Florida, Chapter of the Rough Riders. A special thanks to General Charles Spicola and Captain Robert Martin for their assistance and tour through the Tampa, Florida, Chapter's Rough Rider Museum.

The people of Panama shall forever have a special place in my heart, next to Orfelinato San Jose de Malambo. A thank-you also goes to the family of Princess Maria in Panama City, Panama, for acting as my tour guide while visiting the many historical sites that the city has to offer.

Prologue

My name is Charles Santana—Charlie to my friends. I am the bookkeeper for Mascotte Mercantile, which is located on the northwest corner of Lafayette and Florida Streets here in Tampa. I have been asked by the *Tampa Times* to write about my experiences in the Spanish-American War, specifically my tenure with the First United States Volunteer Cavalry Regiment—the Rough Riders, as we were nicknamed.

Pach's is a small diner located on Franklin Street just a short distance away from my office. It is named after its founder, Pach, although Cathy runs the place now. Every Tuesday night I meet some friends of mine, and we talk about how we can solve all of the problems that exist in the world. Eventually, we get around to that war and that damn hill. Fifteen years have passed since our journey to Cuba; however, I can still see it just as if it were yesterday. Those haunting memories dance across my mind nightly.

Robert Martin is a former Rough Rider, who joins me there on a regular basis. He was my sergeant and squad leader in Cuba and one of only a few who had prior military experience when he joined up. At six foot two, 250 pounds, and with an attitude to go along with his physical stature, he is a bull of a man and a natural leader. We still call him Sarge. He has a dark side to him that I cannot figure out; it's from something prior to our Rough Rider days.

Cole Scudder is another former Rough Rider, who meets with us nearly every week. He is a quiet, reserved, stocky man, who is strong as an ox with a heart of gold. He is a man who you can count on to cover your back, as he did mine several times in Cuba. We started calling him Scooter back in San Antonio.

The three of us put our heads together and even talked with some of our companions, who were there with us in Cuba trying to make sure our memories had not lapsed; heck, we even talked to Teddy Roosevelt before the first article came out. President Roosevelt loaned me his diary, which is a daily log of his conversations and experiences during this "splendid little war," as one of the reporters described our venture.

A few of the other regulars that we meet at Pach's are David, Ron, Bob, Dennis, Vince, and Art. They were not there those months in the mosquito-infested land; however, their eyes sure light up when we get on a roll, laughing at each other, and thanking God that we made it out of there alive, since so many others did not.

Serving in the Rough Riders has allowed us to form a special bond and a unique relationship that shall be with us for the rest of our lives. My wife calls us the "ROMEO" group. We had to explain to Bob that it means "really old men eating out" and not some stud group looking for opportunities.

As a boy growing up in San Antonio, Texas, the Wild West brought many opportunities to me—some good and some best not to speak of. My father was a vaquero, a Mexican cowboy, working for one of the local cattle barons. My mother had her hands full trying to keep us kids in line when we went to school and to church.

When the First United States Volunteer Cavalry Regiment set up camp in San Antonio and started recruiting, I was excited about joining. It was the natural thing for me to do, plus I did not want to herd cattle for a living. My mother did not like the idea of me going off to some foreign land to fight some war that she did not understand. My father gave me his blessing after a long discussion outside of our home over a campfire and a couple of beers.

That is also when he dropped the news on me that he was moving our family to Tampa, Florida. He had been hired by the Carey Dairy as a foreman. We talked more, and I agreed with my parents that Tampa would be a better life for my younger sister and brother.

This story is not about me, my accomplishments, or the friends that I lost in that war. It is a story about a man whose personal life had been shattered and destroyed. It is a story about a man but for whom I would not be here writing this story and had he not had been there with us or for us on that damn hill.

I will never forget that day when he arrived in San Antonio. We were all in the pasture attacking hay bales with a knife attached to a make-believe wooden rifle. I had heard the stories, the old wives' tales, about him and his Indian partner. I had read several of the periodicals on him, especially in Sunday school. No one at the Mission had ever talked about him or that day that changed him. I thought that he was the imaginary hero of some eastern journalist. When he rode through the gate at the Mission, I felt every muscle in my body tighten up. A cool breeze passed over us on that hot, humid Texas day as we stood there watching him.

PART ONE
TEXAS

Chapter 1

San Antonio, Summer 1870

The only thing worse than the hot Texas sun beating down on you is … well, it is the hot Texas sun beating down on you in the middle of July. You can see the heat waves chasing each other across the open plains as if playing a game with your eyes and in your mind. In the distance you hear the whistle of a steam locomotive screaming for water as it nears the depot.

The train depot is usually located on the outskirts of town and requires a good horse and buggy ride to reach. Most visitors to the depot travel from a distant farm or ranch to meet family or friends. This day is different. This train is different. This train does not carry the usual goods from the eastern cities or people looking to start a new life or supplies for the San Antonio markets. This train's cargo is God's precious gift. This train brings children from the eastern orphanages. These children are no longer wanted and have no place to go or stay.

Loading children onto a train and shipping them out of Boston and New York is a program designed to reduce the already overburdened child services of the larger eastern cities while attempting to find suitable homes and accommodations for these children in the Midwest, West, and in the South. These efforts are called Orphan Trains.

The first Orphan Train was in 1854; however, by the late 1860s, the trains mainly carried orphans of soldiers who had died in the American Civil War. In time, many parents gave up their children for placement because the other parent may have died or they simply could not afford to care for the child.

These trains continued on a monthly basis for the next fifty-plus years as the program sought new towns and cities to visit. The majority of the children had good experiences, although there are always a few who do not fare as well as the others.

Visitors to the depot are gathering in a nearby warehouse. They are not there to greet friends or welcome relatives. Some are there to bring a new child into their family, while others are seeking orphans to work their farms, their ranches, their stores, and their markets. The American Civil War may have ended slavery, but servitude is alive and well.

The Orphan Train has now settled into its resting place and is taking on its liquid energy as its cargo is being led into a nearby cattle-auction house that has been modified this day into an orphan-auction house. These children march into an unknown future. Some will work hard and prosper, while others will find themselves out on the streets of San Antonio. All of them will cry themselves to sleep this night.

The auction or adoption process starts as one by one the children are brought out onto a stage starting with the oldest, a twelve-year-old boy named Jason. Most of the orphans over twelve years of age are already on their own. Jason is quickly adopted to a rancher and whisked out of sight. One by one, all of the children are adopted and off they go. Sex and race are unimportant because cheap labor is what is for sale here.

Four hours pass from the start of the adoption process until the last child is brought out onto the stage. The auctioneer looks down on this skinny three-year-old boy dressed in a soiled tan shirt with brown trousers being held up by a tweed rope and brown sandals on his feet. The auctioneer reads aloud a note that has accompanied this little boy on his journey.

Dear Friend,

Please have mercy on my son and take him as yours. His father was killed while working at the ship docks in New York. I cannot care for him and his five brothers and sisters. His name is Kenneth Douglas Hardin. His date of birth is November 3, 1867.

God Bless You.

A rancher yells out from the middle of the shrinking crowd, "Who wants to raise an Irish immigrant's three-year-old boy?"

The remaining crowd laughs and starts heading for the exits.

Standing at the back of the warehouse is Sheriff Billy Wayne Chisholm. He has been sheriff in San Antonio for nearly five years, ever since he left the military. Standing next to the sheriff is his friend Father Ortega, a Mexican priest whose Catholic mission is located on the southwest side of the city.

The auctioneer asks for someone—anyone—to please adopt this boy. At his tender age, he will not survive the streets of San Antonio or wherever else he ends up.

The crowd is steadily leaving the warehouse as Sheriff Chisholm turns to his friend and says, "Father, there is something special about that boy; I can feel it."

Sheriff Chisholm raises his right hand high into the air, toward the auctioneer, and waves it from side to side. At six foot three and 220 pounds, he is easily seen, plus the fact that he is the only one interested in adopting this three-year-old towhead.

The sheriff hands two dollars to his friend.

"Father, please care for this boy and never tell him of this day."

Father Ortega completes the adoption paperwork and pays the customary two-dollar fee. Kenneth Douglas Hardin is now in the care of the Mission of the Son of San Antonio. He shall be known as Kenneth Douglas of Texas, born November 3, 1867.

All of the day's business has been completed as Father Ortega takes young Kenneth by the hand and leads him to a covered wagon. The boy is emotionless. He is a three-year-old boy abandoned by his mother six months ago. Those tears and that pain have all but left him. The memories of the companionship of brothers and sisters have also deserted his memory.

A blank stare imprints itself onto the face of this boy as Father Ortega lifts him onto the bench of the wagon and then climbs aboard himself. Neither of them is aware of the amazing journey that awaits the two of them.

Chapter 2

Father Ortega had arrived in San Antonio just prior to the American Civil War. He had been ordained in 1859 in Mexico City and at the age of twenty was the youngest priest in the New World. He was sent to San Antonio to assist Father Garcia, who ran the Mission of the Son. Church attendance and activity had greatly diminished over the past several years.

Father Garcia retired in 1865 and returned to Mexico City, leaving Father Ortega in charge of the Mission and all of the responsibilities that accompany it. He was equal to the task. He had grand ideas for the century-old adobe Mission.

Scanning the church grounds, just as he had when he first arrived, he sees an old adobe church and bell tower, a pole barn (without walls) for storing hay and supplies, and two old, run-down, makeshift homes.

His idea is to turn the Mission into a self-supporting rancho. He wants to bring in vaqueros to herd cattle left by the Spanish explorers. The Mission could also raise goats and sheep. Wild Spanish mustangs could be rounded up, broken, and sold to the military garrison at the local fort. In order to raise crops to feed the people at the Mission, Ortega wants also to bring in Mexican farmers, who were trying to escape a dictator, and he hopes to attract sharecroppers from the Southern American states, who wanted to make a fresh start. The Mission could sell the extra produce at the local farmers' market.

His most prized idea is to establish the Mission as an orphanage. He has solicited the help of Rose Garcia, Father Garcia's niece, who lives in San Antonio with her husband and attends church at the Mission. She had taught Sunday school for her uncle and teaches English to newly arriving Mexican immigrants.

Father Ortega is already friends with the new sheriff, and Sheriff Chisholm has introduced him to the local military commander and supply quartermaster at the fort.

There is a lot of work that needed attention at the Mission, and Father Ortega is ready to get started.

Chapter 3

"Mr. Yang! Mr. Yang!" Father Ortega shouts as he approaches the pole barn.

Mr. Yang, a forty-five-year-old Chinese immigrant, steps from the barn and waves his left hand high in the air. He was taken in by Father Ortega two years ago to "help with church activities." In actuality, Mr. Yang would not accept a handout, so he started cleaning the church and the barn area and has never left.

He refuses to sleep in one of the Mission's homes because he is used to sleeping under the stars. He says that the beds are just too soft for him, so he sleeps in the hay loft in the upstairs portion of the pole barn. In fact, neither he nor Father Ortega stay in either of the homes, which are in much need of repair, and Father Ortega prefers to live in the back of the church office.

As the covered wagon draws nearer, Mr. Yang notices the little boy seated on the bench of the wagon.

"Father, we have a visitor?"

"No, Mr. Yang, this young man has come to live with us."

With a confused look on his face, Mr. Yang says, "But, Father, we can barely feed two mouths, much less three."

The wagon stops just inside of the barn, and Father Ortega places the guide reins on the floor next to his feet and looks over to Mr. Yang.

"God will help us, for we must help this child. Mr. Yang, this is Kenneth Douglas of Texas. Please help him from the wagon."

Mr. Yang walks over to the right side of the wagon and lifts the little boy out and sets him onto the ground. A smile crosses his face as young Kenneth stands there looking up at him—his bright blue eyes watching his every move, his white towhead hair hanging down in his dust-covered face.

"Mr. Yang, please prepare a place for Kenneth. He will need to stay here near you until we can repair the homes. We have our first orphan!"

Father Ortega grabs from the wagon some supplies that he had bought in town and starts walking toward the church.

Kenneth stands there and watches Father Ortega leave him; he has watched so many do that to him over the past six months.

Mr. Yang walks over to the young man and takes him by the hand and leads him to the back of the barn and stops next to a barrel that is filled to the top with water. He picks up the little boy and throws him into the barrel—clothes and all. Grabbing a sandstone bar that he uses for soap, Yang starts scrubbing Kenneth from head to toe. All the while, the little boy is fighting and screaming.

Father Ortega hears the commotion, comes running from the church, and stops, sliding in his tracks and laughing.

"Mr. Yang, these are the first sounds that I have heard from Mr. Kenneth."

Chapter 4

Mornings come early at the Mission. Mr. Yang is up at 4:00 AM every morning because there are cows that need to be milked, chickens that have to be fed, and other animals that need attention. The animals always come first and before any breakfast or other chores are started.

Kenneth is nestled in his bed of straw in the upper section of the pole barn when he is awakened from his best night's sleep in some time. Young Kenneth has been with the Mission for over a year now and is about to enter into a structured lifestyle that will guide him throughout the rest of his days.

Each day starts the same; they get up at four to tend the animals, then breakfast, and then chores. Kenneth works side by side with Mr. Yang as best he can for his age. Father Ortega brings their meals to the barn, and the three of them pray and eat together.

Father Ortega lights a candle at night and instructs Kenneth in his lessons: reading, writing, arithmetic, and his Catholic studies—all first in English, then Spanish.

Mr. Yang also has lessons for Kenneth. Unknown to Father Ortega, Kenneth is learning the ways of Kung Fu from a Chinese master. He is also being taught Mandarin Chinese.

This schedule remains constant for years and will not change except for Saturdays and Sundays. Saturday mornings are a "go to town" business day for Father Ortega, and on occasion, young Kenneth is allowed to go but only after the majority of his chores have been completed. Mr. Yang always tells Father Ortega that he has, indeed, completed his daily tasks whether he has or not.

Sundays are very busy at the Mission. The animals have to be attended to, then the daily chores, then preparation for Sunday services. Sundays excite young Kenneth for two reasons. Sunday morning service means the ringing of the church bell. Mr. Yang always takes Kenneth up into the bell tower and, on occasion, allows him to assist in the ringing of the bell.

He explains the process to Kenneth: "You have to use your body weight as a counter measure to move the bell housing back and forth so the hammer can strike the interior sides of the housing, thus the ringing of the bell."

The rope used to pull the housing has broken and has been replaced with the lead from a bull whip. In order to grip the lead, they need to wear gloves; otherwise, the lead will shred their hands. Mr. Yang always leaves a pair of gloves in the tower next to a large piece of candle wax.

"You need to peel a piece of the wax off and place it into each of your ears, or you could go deaf from the sound of the bell," he tells Kenneth.

Sunday afternoon means the gathering for a feast. Two dozen or more families from nearby ranches and farms on the southwest side of San Antonio meet around a lone oak tree and visit with one another. There is always a cow or pig being roasted over an open pit, and sometimes both are prepared depending on how many families attend church that morning. The ladies spread side servings out onto a large makeshift table while the men attend to the roasting. Everyone is dressed in their Sunday best.

Mr. Yang never attends these gatherings but says he has unfinished work that needs his attention. He just does not feel comfortable at these social gatherings.

Rose Garcia makes sure Kenneth has something to wear, either hand-me-downs or something she has stitched for him. She is pregnant with her first child, but nonetheless, she cares for Kenneth like a surrogate mother.

This is a special Sunday. Kenneth is now four years old, and Sheriff Chisholm wants to meet him. Sheriff Chisholm and Father Ortega have kept their secret between themselves. Neither Rose nor Mr. Yang knows where Kenneth has come from or what his birth name is.

"Kenneth, come here please!" Father Ortega shouts toward the little man.

The little boy's eyes light up as he looks in their direction. He starts running toward the two men with his towhead white hair flying as he hurries across the yard.

"Yes, Father, I'm coming."

"Kenneth, I would like to introduce Sheriff Chisholm to you."

"Hi there, partner," the sheriff says as Kenneth leans his head back, looking up to the face of this giant of a man.

"Hello, sir, I'm pleased to meet you."

Chapter 5

Mexico experiences decades of internal turmoil after the Treaty of Guadalupe Hidalgo turned over Mexican lands to the United States, thus ending the Mexican-American War. The invasion attempt by France and the reign of Maximilian are at an end, and with the death of Benito Juarez, the Mexican people are facing many challenges from President Diaz.

President Diaz has become the dictator that the Mexican people fear. He has established the Rurales, an armed and mobile police force made up mostly of bandits. They police the countryside and seek out persons opposed to Diaz's rule—often killing them and seldom taking prisoners. The military supports these expeditions and often assists in hunting down so-called dissidents.

The freedoms the Mexican people have enjoyed under the rule of President Benito Juarez are fading quickly. Small farmers are no longer allowed to own their own land without a title, which is a document that usually eludes them.

Religious freedoms are also being restricted, and properties owned by the Catholic Church are being seized by the government. One of the most prized religious objects is a Latin cross that was crafted in the middle of the 1500s in the city of Santo Domingo. The cross is eighteen inches tall and eight inches wide. It is rumored to be made of solid gold with two five-carat rubies atop the patibulum on each side. It found a resting place in the Church of San Bernardo when it opened in 1636 in the center of Mexico City.

After the cross disappeared from the church, the Mexican government has stopped at nothing to locate it. The cross is worth a fortune when melted down into its original state. All of the treasures that the people and church cherish are disappearing, having been confiscated or destroyed. The iron fist of the dictator wants no distractions; the people shall worship and praise his likeness.

Bandits of all types—the out-of-work cowboy, the outlaw, and even the civilized Indian—are scouring the countryside, seeking the cross from Mexico City to the new territory of California. Nearly every church and every mission is searched and ransacked by these desperadoes. Lives are lost, and some are sacrificed for what has become known as "The Symbol of the Peasant." The cross continues to elude the Mexican government.

The border area between Mexico and the United States quickly expands in population, with many Mexican nationals moving into south Texas and other states that adjoin the border. Mexican ranchers and farmers are fleeing their homes in greater numbers, seeking some type of work to support their families.

The economy of the region is changing as well, as cattle drives become an important activity in Texas, stimulated by the increasing demands for beef from the eastern and northern cities. Cattle ranchers who own the herds hire immigrant Mexican vaqueros to move their cattle north to Abilene, where the Missouri-Kansas-Texas Railway has completed a line from Abilene to the Chicago slaughterhouses. The railroad has also built stockyards for holding the cattle until they can be loaded and shipped back east. These cattle drives become routine and are an economic windfall for the cattle barons.

The cattle drives usually start near San Antonio's Chisholm Trail and travel north to Fort Griffin, then across the Red River and through Oklahoma to Abilene. San Antonio is quickly becoming the hub of activity for the beef industry. Several kinds of support businesses are opening in and around the San Antonio area, and Mexican immigrants find jobs to support their families.

There is even talk that the railroads will expand. The Union Pacific Railroad is trying to link up with the Missouri-Kansas-Texas Railway somewhere around the Fort Worth area. It plans to expand a southern route west to California, while the Missouri-Kansas-Texas Railway wants to expand north toward Canada and east toward Houston.

Father Ortega has foreseen these possibilities several years ago. He and Sheriff Chisholm often speak of the changes that are coming and how they will affect their peaceful community.

The Mexican population explosion is in full swing along with the arrival of drifter gunfighters, who have appeared as a result of the end of the American Civil War. They are out-of-work gunslingers, who are looking to make a name for themselves at anyone's expense. Writers of dime novels and for the eastern periodicals make heroes out of the gunfighters. The big cities of the East and Europe are starved for stories of the adventures of the Wild West. The stores cannot keep the small periodicals in stock. In New York City, stage play after stage play begins to depict the West, and in decades to come, Wild West shows will sell out all across the East Coast and Europe.

Chapter 6

The El Paso Salt Flats are located on the far west side of Texas at the Guadalupe Mountains. They are the remains of an old riverbed and mean the economic survival of the Mexican border population. People travel hundreds of miles for the salt product.

This had gone on for decades, until the Anglos moved into the El Paso Valley region. The Anglos are attempting to gain title to the area. This has started a heated struggle between them and the Mexican community, which is now faced with the possibility of having to pay taxes for collecting the salt.

This action has upset many in the Mexican community, for they believe that the Treaty of Guadalupe Hidalgo establishes the salt lakes as public property. They also feel that the Anglos are exploiting the natural resources that belong to the Mexicans.

Father Ortega has asked Hector Garcia, a member of the Mexican border community and an experienced vaquero, to bring his family and come and live at the Mission. Garcia has led several cattle drives from San Antonio north to Abilene and the slaughterhouses in Kansas City, and he has also guided wagon trains across Texas to the El Paso Salt Flats. He is excited over the prospect of moving his family to the Mission. He and Father Ortega have already agreed upon certain aspects of how to establish the rancho, and Ortega has said that the vaquero could be a valuable asset to the Mission.

Garcia does not like leaving his wife, Rose, and their daughter, Marie, alone while he leaves San Antonio for months at a time on cattle drives. He hopes they are safe; however, being gone from his wife and five-year-old daughter does not set well with him while he is out on the open range.

On his next trip, Hector arrives in El Paso with ten Conestoga wagons and plans to load up on the salt and return to San Antonio as quickly as he can. As the wagon train enters the valley, Hector notices several men on the roadway with rifles. This alarms him and the other wagon operators, who have joined him on this salt expedition.

The wagons are stopped at a makeshift road block, and Hector is instructed to pay a salt tax of fifty dollars per wagon. This tax is outrageous and not affordable. He attempts to explain to the men that he has made this journey numerous times without having to pay a tax. He does not understand why he has to this time.

Hector is speaking with one of the men in charge when a cowboy standing nearby raises his rifle and strikes him across the forehead, knocking him to the ground. He attempts to regain his wits as his companions rush to his aid. Several gunshots ring out, and Hector and two of his men fall dead.

The remaining men raise their hands in surrender and are allowed to gather the three bodies. They load them into the first wagon and leave to return to San Antonio.

Word quickly spreads throughout El Paso and into San Elizario. The Mexican community is outraged over the actions taken by this gang of gunmen, who have set up at the entrance to the salt flats claiming ownership to their property.

The El Paso Salt War has begun, and there will be many deaths on both sides. This war will come to an end in just a few weeks when United States Cavalry troops and a squad of Texas Rangers claim the land for Texas.

Rose Garcia is devastated over the death of her husband. Not knowing what the future holds for her or her daughter, she turns to Father Ortega.

Father Ortega and Rose complete the plans for the rancho that Hector was developing. Rose must contact the men that Hector was planning to bring on board. She has to be strong, knowing she will be without her husband and that her daughter will grow up without her father.

Rose has asked one thing of Father Ortega. She has asked that Kenneth come and live with her and Marie in one of the homes. She does not like the idea of him sleeping in that barn. He needs a real family environment. Father Ortega agrees, and a partnership is established.

Chapter 7

The time has come for the Mission of the Son to put the development plan into full operation. Father Ortega has been in charge of the Mission for several years, and Kenneth is now ten years old—old enough to help with some of the physical labor instead of just carrying small items around the Mission for Mr. Yang.

Father Ortega has to leave the mission and go to a nearby ranch to attempt to mediate a dispute between a rancher and a farmer over water rights. Sheriff Chisholm has said that he will go by the mission and check in on his friends until Father Ortega will return in a couple of days. He takes every opportunity to see Kenneth that he can, plus he loves Rose's cooking.

Rose has moved into one of the homes on the mission property. Mr. Yang and Kenneth are hard at work, attempting to repair the roof and the other infrastructure needs on that home, while the other one will have to wait its turn. It is Marie's job keep to the two of them supplied with water on this hot day, and she takes great pride in that job.

Mr. Yang and Kenneth climb down from the roof, and there is Marie with a bucket full of water. Both of them take a big gulp and even pour some over their hot sweaty bodies. Kenneth takes an extra pail and throws it on Marie. The chase is on. Rose and Mr. Yang stand there laughing as the little seven-year-old Marie chases Kenneth toward and into the bell tower, where they soon disappear. Rose and Mr. Yang are laughing so hard their sides are hurting, and tears are running down their faces.

Kenneth runs up the steps to the top of the first floor with Marie just a short distance behind him. He sprints up the next two flights of stairs until he reaches the top of the bell tower and stops next to the whip lead used to pull the bell housing. Marie soon catches up to him and runs straight at him, like a bull charging the matador's cape. He is laughing and not paying attention when Marie runs right up to him, plants both of her hands into his chest, and pushes him.

Falling backward, all he can do is to grab a hold of the bull whip lead. Holding onto the lead without gloves soon begins to cut into his hands. Kenneth wraps his legs around the lead in an attempt to steady himself, but the lead soon starts cutting into his stomach like a razor blade on a virgin face, and he cannot hold on. He falls three stories, first landing on his feet to break his fall, but then still hitting the back of his head on the hard wood flooring. He lays there motionless as Marie looks over the edge and screams in horror.

Rose and Mr. Yang hear the shrieking screams coming from the bell tower. Marie's screams are like that of a bobcat at night—a high pitched sound that cuts through the silence as if it never existed. They began to run immediately toward the bell tower.

Sheriff Chisholm is just entering the mission property when he sees the two of them running across the grounds. He puts his horse into a fast gallop, and the three of them come together at the bell-tower entrance.

Rose is the first to enter the tower, and she sees Kenneth lying on the floor on his stomach with his face turned to the right; both of his arms are spread out away from the sides of his body. Blood runs from under him at a steady pace. Marie is still screaming when Mr. Yang and Sheriff Chisholm enter the bell tower.

Sheriff Chisholm quickly runs back to his horse and removes a blanket attached to the rear of his saddle. Mr. Yang and Rose attempt to sit Kenneth up when they notice a gash from his belt line to his chest. Blood runs out profusely.

Sheriff Chisholm runs back into the bell tower and lifts an unconscious Kenneth up and wraps him in the blanket.

"I'm taking him to see Doc Wilson; he's over at the Morris farm just a few miles away. Mr. Yang, please make sure Marie is okay."

Mr. Yang runs up the three levels of stairs to a hysterical Marie, picks her up, and hugs her in an attempt to comfort her. He then carries her down to Rose. Tears are chasing one another down Marie's face because she believes she has seriously hurt her friend.

The horses are quickly harnessed and hitched to the wagon. Mr. Yang, Rose, and Marie start to the Morris farm.

Sheriff Chisholm is riding as fast as his horse can carry the two of them. It may only be a few miles away, but he is attempting to hold onto Kenneth and slow the bleeding while also riding his horse through an open pasture. What would normally take just minutes is turning into a dozen minutes at a full gallop. He arrives at the farm yelling at the top of his voice for the doctor. Mr. Morris steps from inside and motions for Doc Wilson to come outside. Doc Wilson is there to attend to the Morris's newborn baby.

"Hurry, Doc. He's hurt bad," Sheriff Chisholm says as he dismounts his horse with Kenneth unconscious in his arms.

They take the young man into the house and lay him across the kitchen table. Doc Wilson sends Mr. Morris to get buckets of water while he has the sheriff push down on the wound to slow the bleeding. Doc Wilson retrieves his medical bag from the back bedroom, and immediately he goes to work on Kenneth.

He orders Sheriff Chisholm to go out and greet the arriving family members, "Keep them outside so I can work on Kenneth without interruption."

Mr. Yang, Rose, Marie, and Sheriff Chisholm are all outside waiting when Doc Wilson and Mr. Morris step out to speak with them. Doc Wilson is wiping sweat from his forehead as he looks to the four of them.

"Well, I used all the catgut I had to sew him up. It's wait and see now. He's lost a lot of blood."

Marie leans over into her mother's arms, still crying, to seek her comfort.

The three of them stay at the Morris farm that night, while Mr. Yang returns to the Mission. There is always work that has to be completed, regardless of the situation.

The Morris roosters start early this day, before sunrise, as if they know that troubled hearts are visiting their farm.

Marie walks over to see Kenneth. who is still lying on the table and covered with a blanket. She leans right over him just inches away and stares at his face, her long black hair hanging to each side of his face. Kenneth opens one eye and looks at her as a smile crosses his face.

Marie smiles back as the others awaken to her apologies for hurting him. Rose gets out of a chair by the fireplace and quickly moves to Kenneth to hug him while crying tears of joy and thanking the Lord for bringing her boy back. Sheriff Chisholm joins them as the Morrises come out of their bedroom, all with smiles covering their faces. Kenneth reaches his right hand to Marie and holds hers, telling her how sorry he is for throwing the water on her. All of them laugh when Rose tells Kenneth now he has no excuse for not practicing on the piano with Marie—the church choir needs the two of them on the piano.

Kenneth will have a two-inch-wide scar from his belt line to his chest for the rest of his life.

After the accident, Kenneth and Sheriff Chisholm spend Saturdays together, and the sheriff promises to teach Kenneth how to ride a horse and, someday, how to shoot a firearm.

A special bond has formed between Kenneth and Marie. They have become inseparable. When Marie finishes her chores with her mother, she then goes looking for Kenneth. Each day, he finishes his chores and starts looking for her. Even when the construction started on the other homes and the barracks for the orphans, Marie stands right there with that all-familiar bucket of water.

Father Ortega has Mr. Yang replace the bull-whip lead with a forty-foot rope.

Chapter 8

The Mexican and Texas communities are not the only ones affected by the unrest that is sweeping across the southwestern territories. Mexican people are being displaced from their lands just as the American Civil War had displaced many Americans from their homes.

The Apache Indians are also trying to survive as a people. They had migrated to the Texas Panhandle in the mid-1500s from their homes in Canada. A spiritual and peaceful band of people who hunt for food and raised crops, they learned to fight and become warriors with the arrival of the Spanish explorers. The Apache had moved to south Texas, fleeing the Comanche warriors who also migrated much along the same path as they had.

The Apaches sought shelter and protection from the Comanche in the Spanish missions. With virtually no place to run, they became refugees looking for help and a home. The priests and monks who ran the missions then treated the Apache like slaves, working them from sunrise to sunset. Many of the Apache died from disease and malnutrition.

In the 1800s, the Apache Indians moved out of the missions and separated into two groups. One group left Texas and moved to New Mexico under a chieftain who named his band the Mescalero Apaches. Geronimo, the Mescalero chieftain, became a folk hero to the Apache nation and fought the European settlers and their armies for several years before being forced onto a New Mexico reservation.

Grandfather, another Apache chieftain took the remaining Apaches, called the Lipan, to the Rio Grande and set up camp with the Kickapoo Indians between the Mexican and Texas settlers. Their way of life was coming to an end by the late 1800s. Stalking Wolf, the son of Grandfather, has actually left the band and works for the Texas Rangers as a scout. He is assigned to the San Antonio office, working with the local sheriff. He has not forgotten his early childhood days at the Catholic missions. He often visits with Father Ortega, and they have struck up a unique friendship.

Mexican President Diaz has sent his Rurales and soldiers into the Kickapoo territory along the Rio Grande to raid the Indian villages and kill the Apache men, women, and children. They are directed to kill as many as they can regardless of age or sex.

President Diaz blames the Lipan Apache Indians for hiding political dissidents and resistance fighters, who he believes are trying to overthrow the regional governors. These mass killings will continue for several weeks until the United States Cavalry responds and moves the remaining survivors to New Mexico and unites them with the Mescalero Apaches on a private reservation.

Grandfather and his family do not make the journey to New Mexico. He travels to San Antonio and joins Stalking Wolf at the Mission of the Son. An agreement between the US Cavalry and Father Ortega has allowed Grandfather and his family to live and work at the Mission. Stalking Wolf moves his family to the Mission as well. He continues his scouting work with the Texas Rangers.

The Lipan Apache Indians are known as master horse whispers, and this will be a great asset to Father Ortega and his plans for the Mission. He greets Grandfather and the Indian leader's family with an outstretched hand:

"Grandfather, I understand the misgivings you have and bad treatment that you and your people have suffered not only from the Comanche and the Mexican government, but also from my predecessors among the clergy. However, in time, I hope to change your opinion of us. I ask that you and your family stay here at the Mission of the Son and treat our home as yours."

Grandfather extends his hand in friendship to Father Ortega and says, "My family will stay here with you; we shall work and earn our stay."

Stalking Wolf and his family are also given their own home. They are now part of the Mission's family.

Chapter 9

Sheriff Chisholm has kept his promise to teach Kenneth how to ride a horse. The Indians at the Mission have also taught him their whispering techniques of horse breaking. Kenneth has become quite the horseman after working with Stalking Wolf on a regular basis, whenever the Apache scout came back into San Antonio after a mission for the Texas Rangers. Kenneth learned all the tricks that he could, like mounting a horse from a running start.

He has now become an outstanding horseman, except for the time that Marie loosened the saddle just before he attempted his running mount.

Kenneth and Marie go for rides in the early morning hours in order to watch Mother Nature and her creatures awaken to a new day. Kenneth is always trying to impress Marie; she just rolls her eyes and turns her head away smiling but making sure that he cannot see her face. He is her hero, but she is not about to let him know that secret. He loves everything about her: her coal-black hair that hangs down to her mocha-colored shoulders and her big brown eyes that make his heart pound. But it is her smile that lights up his life. She smiles at him, and a spark jumps from her smile toward him, and his heart melts.

One morning, they come upon a hole in the ground that has obviously been dug by some creature in the not-too-distant past. They dismount and walk toward this hole, and they soon see a mother rabbit and her babies. They stop and watch the joy that is before them. Marie walks back to the horses while Kenneth stands there watching this young family. She reaches into one of the saddlebags and removes some pieces of bread. She always carries bread slices with her just in case she has the chance to cross paths with some of nature's creatures. She also reaches under Kenneth's horse and loosens the saddle strap that holds the saddle onto the back of his horse.

After leaving the bread just a few feet away from the mother rabbit, it is time to go. Kenneth helps Marie up onto her horse, and then it is his turn to mount his in a fashion that she has come to know all too well. Kenneth runs as fast as he can, and with a leap high into the air, Marie slaps the rear of his horse just as he lands onto the unsecured saddle. His horse takes off in one direction as Kenneth and his saddle go in the other direction.

Marie is laughing so loud and hard that she cannot control her tears as they run down her face. She is so caught up in her laughter and proud of herself that she has not noticed him laying on the ground and not moving. He is lying on his left side with his right leg over the dislodged saddle and his cowboy hat covering his face. She jumps down from her horse and runs over to him, her mind racing back to that day in the bell tower.

"Kenneth! Kenneth!" she shouts as she runs to him and drops to her knees.

She rolls him over very gently to face her as fear fills her mind. Kenneth looks up to Marie, smiling from ear to ear and trying not to laugh at the trick he has just pulled upon her. Realizing that he is just fine, she reaches back as far as she can with her right hand and slaps his chest as they share a laugh.

Kenneth slowly reaches up to her, and with a hand on each shoulder, he pulls her down to him and gently kisses her soft lips. Marie jerks away from him and stares back down at him. She leans down to him as their lips meet again in a passionate moment. He holds her close to him as they lay there together. He can feel her heart beating faster and faster against his chest. Her skin is so soft, and her beauty is irresistible. Their love has now exposed itself to each other—a love they knew of but were afraid to share.

Kenneth thinks that it was a good idea that six months ago he moved into the barracks that they have built for the other orphans.

Chapter 10

Neither Rose nor Father Ortega like the idea of guns; however, both of them are aware that the knowledge of handling a gun will be necessary for survival in the Wild West, which San Antonio has become a part of.

Sheriff Chisholm explains the internal workings of the handgun to Kenneth with Marie sitting right by his side.

"The six bullets are loaded with the lead end, the smaller end, away from you and the larger circular end toward you. The hammer is cocked, and the trigger is pulled so that the hammer strikes down upon the center of the circular end, causing a small explosion, thus sending the lead out of the barrel and toward its intended target.

"In order to sight in onto a target, you have to line the front sight with the rear sight. The front blade sight has to be lined in the center of the rear U-shaped sight."

Kenneth and Marie sit and listen intently to each word that Sheriff Chisholm speaks. Their eyes are wide open, as if he is telling them of a great adventure story from his military days.

"The trigger has to be pulled back in a single motion and not jerked. Jerking the trigger will push the front sight to one side or another and pull the gun off line from the intended target."

Sheriff Chisholm holds his handgun in front of them, not loaded; the two youngsters move closer to him and close together with their full attention on the handgun—neither of them realizes that they sit touching one another in the presence of a third party.

Kenneth practices each day, and when he and Marie go for their morning rides, she also practices shooting. Kenneth assists her in holding the handgun by wrapping his arms around her. Marie can fire the handgun just fine without his help, both of them know this, but this is an opportunity for him to hug her and for her to be hugged by him.

Kenneth becomes a sharpshooter with any firearm that he picks up. Sheriff Chisholm is amazed at how fast he can remove the pistol from its left-handed holster and fire dead center on target every single time, whether he is on foot or on horseback. With a Winchester rifle, he is even more deadly. He can pick off any target from seventy-five yards away. The steady hands that Mr. Yang helped him develop as a child are paying off now.

"Never draw a gun unless you intend on using it" is a statement beat into Kenneth's head every day by Sheriff Chisholm.

Saturday night means dinner at Rose's house, a tradition they established back when Rose first settled at the Mission. Father Ortega, Sheriff Chisholm, Kenneth, Marie, and Rose all gather together and share good times. Sheriff Chisholm views Kenneth as a mature man, although he is only eighteen years old, and he surprises the others when he brings up the subject of Kenneth becoming his deputy.

"San Antonio is growing, and I need another deputy. Besides, if he and Marie intend on getting married, he needs a steady job."

It's not clear who is blushing more from embarrassment, Kenneth or Marie. Father Ortega stares at the two young people, holding his glass of water in midair, his mouth dropping open and speechless for the first time since the sheriff has known him. Rose actually drops her glass of water onto the floor. No one makes a sound; you can almost hear the moon racing across the night sky, it is so quiet.

Kenneth takes a deep breath and looks around the room.

With his face now flushed with embarrassment, he speaks up, "Well, I guess the time has come for me to express my desire to have Marie as my wife sometime in the future, if that will meet with your approval, Miss Rose, and if Maria accepts me as her future husband."

Marie jumps from the table and lands in his arms, which causes the chair that he is seated in to fall to the floor with her atop of him.

"Yes! Yes! Yes!" she shouts, kissing him and hugging him.

She then looks back over her right shoulder to her mother and says with a big smile, "If it is okay with you, Mother."

Rose begins to cry as those tears of joy have returned and blessed her this day. Father Ortega is so excited he is again speechless. Sheriff Chisholm looks around with a dumbfounded expression.

"I thought everyone knew that they are in love."

The next week, Kenneth arrives ready and willing his first day, dressed in a long-sleeve tan shirt, tan pants, black riding boots, and wearing a white hat. On his left hip is a brand new Colt .45, a Texas six–shooter, a gift from the sheriff to his new deputy.

The new deputy is reluctant to take the job of carrying a handgun and enforcing laws that he is not sure that he understands the meaning of himself. However, Deputy Douglas is up to the task and looks forward to the training phase with his mentor, and at the age of eighteen, he is eager to learn all that he can. He will need the pay if he is to start a family with Marie.

Sheriff Chisholm and Kenneth are soon walking down the center of Main Street. Like a proud father with his chest stuck out and a smile upon his face, Chisholm makes it a point to speak to everyone who is outside on this morning, just so they can see his new partner.

Sitting on a chair outside of the Menger Hotel is a former army buddy turned bounty hunter, Robert Martin. He makes eye contact with Sheriff Chisholm as they nod their heads to each other, a sign of respect. The sheriff knows Martin very well but does not like the idea that he brings in his prey dead the majority of the time, which makes them "easier to handle," he says.

Robert Martin is younger than Sheriff Chisholm by several years. He is from Pittsburgh, and they both served in the same cavalry regiment. Martin left the military in search of Confederate gold in Mexico and gained an infamous reputation as a pistolero. He has an eye for the Spanish ladies and an itch for poker. He is always dressed in black with dual gun holsters that sport silver buttons that line his belt. He has metal taps on the bottoms of his black boots and silver spurs that reflect the sunlight. He wears a black cowboy hat with a silver band. He wants you to know that he is approaching. This day a fifteen-year-old prostitute is at his side.

The new deputy tips his hat to the young lady.

"What are you doing?" the sheriff asks. "Don't upset Martin with that gesture toward his girl. He is a dangerous man."

"We are all God's children," Kenneth replies.

Chapter 11

By 1883, the days of the open range and long cattle drives are coming to an end. Cattle are being herded to train shipping stations. Eastern and European investors are buying up the cattle ranches and using a new invention to block off the open range: barbed wire, which is changing Texas and the West. Cowboys are finding that their days are numbered, and large groups are finding themselves out of work. The new ranch owners pay the cowboys in cash and no longer allow them access to their lands for herding their own cattle.

Cowboys strike against these new owners but to no avail. Many of them find themselves on the streets of San Antonio and in the saloons, trying to make a buck. Eastern and European journalists stage bets on gunfights. Sheriff Chisholm and his deputies attempt to stop these displays but often learn of the matches after the fact or as the challengers are facing off in the middle of the street. The journalists are the true moneymakers here. They document and illustrate these daring displays for their periodicals. Cowboys turned gunslingers crowd the streets, trying to make a name for themselves and at any one's expense.

Sam Bass, a one-time legitimate business entrepreneur turned bank robber, is wanted by the Texas Rangers and is on the run from Pinkerton detectives when he is seen by another of Chisholm's deputies, Deputy Andrew Grimes, entering a tobacco store across the street from the Menger Hotel. Deputy Grimes grew up near San Antonio on one of the local farms and was a childhood friend of Kenneth's. He attended church at the Mission with his family.

He attempts to force Sam Bass and his two gang members to surrender.

"Sam Bass, stop where you are. You are under arrest!"

But Grimes is no match for Bass and his two partners. He is shot dead in the middle of the street.

Deputy Douglas, who is walking around inside of the general store looking for boiled candy for Marie, hears the gunshots down the street and starts running toward his friend.

"Grimes! Grimes!" he shouts.

Sam Bass and the two others turn toward Kenneth as he approaches. Bass fires one shot at Kenneth but misses. Kenneth displays those quick reactions that he learned as a child and draws his .45 as he dives to his right and lands in the dirt street next to a water trough. Two shots ring out—then a third. Bass's two gang members fall dead in the street, and Sam Bass himself is wounded after he manages to mount his horse, but he rides out of town, leaning to his left with his right arm covering his belly.

Kenneth looks over to the hotel, knowing that he has only fired his pistol twice. On the porch stands the bounty hunter Robert Martin with a pistol in his right hand. He stares back to the young deputy and nods his head. Sam Bass was attempting to shoot Kenneth as he mounted his horse when Robert Martin exited the hotel and fired, hitting Bass in the stomach. Bass rode out of town but is found lying in a field the next day by rail workers. He dies the following day.

Martin may have saved Kenneth from certain death that day, but journalists knew they had a new hero in the deputy. The Eastern and European tabloids ignore Martin but go wild with the headlines and stories nonstop about Kenneth:

"An eighteen-year-old orphan boy turned deputy sheriff has stopped the Sam Bass gang from robbing a bank in San Antonio. Neither the Texas Rangers nor the Pinkerton Detective Agency could stop the Sam Bass gang, but the teenage deputy has laid the outlaw gang to rest."

This is the start of the onslaught of reporters who are looking for information on the young deputy. Marie is terrified when she learns of the near-death experience that her love has just encountered. Sheriff Chisholm attempts to calm her and Rose by saying that this type of incident just does not happen that often.

"Tomorrow, the Chinese rail workers are planning a big parade in celebration of their new year. Let's forget about this incident and enjoy the parade," he says, trying to distract them from their worried thoughts.

Father Ortega and Kenneth sit down in the back office of the church.

"Father, I have sinned. I have killed two men today."

"My son," Ortega says with a troubled face as he reaches out a hand and places it upon the shoulder of the trouble teen. "God does not look down on you for taking the lives of the devil's helpers. These were bad men, Satan's assassins, men who have killed and robbed all across Texas. You have saved lives by performing your duty today."

Kenneth leans back and looks up to Father Ortega.

"Thank you, Father. I need your guidance."

The Chinese Lunar New Year parade starts bright and early the next morning with John Wah Chung, an immigrant and political activist, leading a large contingent down the center of Main Street.

The Texas and Pacific Railway has brought nearly three thousand Chinese rail workers to the San Antonio area. The Galveston Railway has employed nearly two thousand Irish rail workers. The Irish are not liked, but the Chinese are disliked even more for their unusual dress, as people who eat strange and peculiar food, and men who wear their hair in pigtails. The Chinese are thought to have taken jobs away from the cowboys after the Strike of 1883 has left many of them unemployed.

Fireworks explode along with cheers and smiles from all of the Chinese who stand along the street side as a large green and yellow dragon with its fearsome face lead many of the parade participants as it weaves from side to side. Gymnasts are performing their acrobatics, jumping and tumbling down the street as well.

Sheriff Chisholm and Kenneth are standing by the hotel watching this magnificent display when several cowboys exit the saloon from across the street and are followed by a handful of journalists. It is obvious that these men have been drinking most of the night with their laughing and carrying on. As the parade draws nearer, one of the cowboys runs out into the street and shoots John Wah Chung several times.

The other cowboys follow him and open fire on the parade goers. Sheriff Chisholm and Kenneth cross the street and reach for their pistols. Kenneth yells to the Chinese in their native language to seek shelter. Gunshots are fired in all directions as the Chinese parade goers run away. Sheriff Chisholm is shot in the right hand as he attempts to draw his pistol.

"Kenneth! I'm hit!" he cries.

The bullet has gone through his hand and into his right leg, sending him to the ground, and he is not able to pull his pistol from its holster. Kenneth is in a gunfight alone against seven cowboys.

Mr. Yang taught him to move quickly and seek cover when outnumbered. That is not an option with the sheriff laying in the middle of the street with only a pile of dirt for protection. Kenneth fires his pistol in rapid succession. He first shoots a cowboy who has turned from the parade and is shooting at the sheriff. One cowboy down, but two others turn and face him with their guns blazing. Kenneth kneels down and then runs and jumps to the ground, does a forward roll, and comes up shooting. Two more dead, but it's four against one now, and Kenneth has used four of his six bullets.

Trying to protect the sheriff, Kenneth rolls across the ground dodging bullets from the four drunken gunmen. He rolls to his right and fires two more shots and somehow finds his targets. He is out of bullets and no time to reload. The other two cowboys are standing in the street, loading their pistols and laughing.

The sheriff uses his left hand to draw and then throw his pistol to Kenneth.

"Kenneth! Here, use my pistol!" he shouts to his new deputy just as the two cowboys finish loading their pistols and start to fire on him.

Kenneth jumps to his right, catches the pistol, and fires back—one cowboy falls to the ground face first in the dirt.

The other cowboy is firing wildly.

"I'm hit!" Kenneth shouts back to the sheriff.

Kenneth is wounded in his right side and right leg. The bullet enters his right leg just below the hip, forcing Kenneth to fall on his right side.

The remaining cowboy runs over to the front of the saloon and grabs the fifteen-year-old prostitute who was with the bounty hunter the other day. He holds his left arm around her neck with her body in front of him as a shield.

The cowboy is firing his pistol, but the young prostitute is screaming in horror and struggling to get free, which forces his aim to go astray.

He yells to her, "Stand still!"

Kenneth sits up in the middle of the street and leans to his right, resting on his elbow. His right leg is extended under his body. He takes a deep breath. and from fifty feet away, fires one shot that finds its target—the cowboy's forehead.

The cowboy falls away; his grip on the young girl is loosened; and she runs to the other ladies inside of the saloon, screaming at the top of her lungs.

The journalists are stunned over the event that has just happened before their eyes. Chinese parade goers rush to aid Kenneth and the sheriff. They are astounded that an Anglo lawman has spoken to them in their native Mandarin language, and they want to help him.

Father Ortega, Rose, and Marie are just arriving into town as this gun battle is ending. Marie jumps from the wagon.

"Kenneth! Kenneth!" she screams as she runs toward him.

Two days in a row, he has been nearly killed. Doc Wilson runs over to the two lawmen. Kenneth is the worse of the two, "but contracted only a flesh wound" according to Doc.

Eastern and European journalists run to the telegraph office and send messages back to their respected papers with the news of the gun battle.

"One day he stops one of the most notorious outlaw gangs in Texas; the next day he saves hundreds of parade goers by outgunning seven gunslingers single-handedly."

He is labeled the "Boy Deputy of San Antonio," a nickname that will stick with him for several years to come.

The following month, there is a celebration in San Antonio, and the governor of Texas presents Kenneth with a hero's badge. Captain Junius Peak of the Texas Rangers attempts to recruit the young lawman, right there on the spot. He even calls upon a mutual friend for assistance. "Stalking Wolf will be your guide, and you will only go on special missions for the Rangers. You should not be involved in these types of incidents again."

Kenneth and Marie discuss the offer from the Rangers. The upside is that there should be no more gun battles in the streets and Stalking

Wolf will be his partner. The downside is being away from each other for weeks at a time. It is Stalking Wolf's promise to Marie that he shall watch out for Kenneth that convinces her that this is the right choice for them. Kenneth accepts the Rangers' offer with the blessing of Sheriff Chisholm, Rose, and Father Ortega.

Chapter 12

Indian Territory was first established by the British, but changes to that agreement have been an on going process by the American government. The Indian Removal Act of 1830 started the relocation, and the infamous Trail of Tears experienced by the Cherokee nation widened the diplomatic gap between the white man and his Indian counterparts. Oklahoma and parts of Arkansas are established as the new territory for Indian settlements. Other tribes like the Delaware, Cheyenne, and some Apache are also forced to relocate to these areas.

The Medicine Lodge Treaty of 1867 attempted to provide the Native Americans with food, clothing, shelter, and guns and ammunition for hunting. In exchange, the Indians were to stop their raids on the wagon trains moving west to seek California gold. White hunters moved into these areas and started killing buffalo herds just for their hides and leaving the remains to rot. The bison herds were becoming extinct, which left the Indians to depend on reservation food rations.

The Native Americans leave the reservations in attempts to regain their freedom. Lack of food and warm clothing also contribute to their distrust of the Indian Affairs Bureau. Cherokee and Comanche raids extend down into the panhandle of Texas and sometimes to the outer reaches of Fort Worth.

Several groups from the Comanche, Southern Cheyenne (the Dog Warriors), and Arapaho join forces under the leadership of Isa-tai (Coyote Dung). Isa-tai is a young warrior of the Quahadi band of Comanche. Isa-tai easily convinces the elders, whose people face starvation, that war against the white man is the only solution. He lays out a plan to attack the white buffalo hunters at Adobe Wells.

Isa-tai and three hundred warriors attack the twenty-eight hunters on a bright July morning in 1886 but to no avail. The hunters are well armed with long-range rifles and hold off the attackers. This defeat sends the majority of the Indians back to the reservation where the US Army restricts their movement. The remaining hostile Indians scatter over the plains of Texas. The Red River War has begun.

Isa-tai returns to the reservation in an attempt to reassemble his army, but Comanche Chief Parker is not impressed with his efforts.

He says, "You have killed many of our young men on your foolish venture. No more will you lead us to slaughter."

Isa-tai and his small group of followers are forced to leave the reservation by the elders. But Isa-tai kidnaps Falling Star, the daughter of Chief Parker, and heads to the Texas Panhandle, the upper region of the Red River.

Texas Ranger Kenneth Douglas and his scout, Stalking Wolf, receive a telegram from Ranger Headquarters that contains new orders of a most urgent matter:

Renegade Indian Isa-tai has kidnapped Comanche Princess Falling Star and is believed to be in the Texas Panhandle region. Your orders are to apprehend Isa-tai and return Princess Falling Star safely to her home. You are to meet up with Colonel Nelson Miles of the US Army at Palo Duro Canyon. You are the only Rangers assigned this task.

"Well, Stalking Wolf, it looks as if we are taking a train ride to North Texas."

"Yes, my friend," Stalking Wolf says as he walks toward the barn to ready their horses and supplies.

Kenneth walks to Marie with the news of his assignment. Standing on the porch outside of her home, Marie looks into the eyes of her true love and with a hand upon each of his shoulders.

"Please use care and return to me."

"I will be okay. Stalking Wolf will see to that."

The two embrace and share a kiss good-bye.

The train ride to Fort Worth takes a day, and the ride by horseback from Fort Worth to the upper Red River region takes another three days. Stalking Wolf knows this area very well. He has tracked many an outlaw into this region.

The US Army's main objective is to encircle the entire region, moving from the north to the south, west to the east while additional cavalry groups approach from the opposite directions. Several encounters have already occurred with the Indians losing many of their warriors.

Stalking Wolf heads straight to Palo Duro Canyon.

"Isa-tai should be in the canyon. It is the only safe place with shelter and water. He can hold off the cavalry from that location as long as he has food."

Ranger Douglas agrees.

Douglas and Stalking Wolf meet Colonel Nelson Miles and discuss the disadvantages they face attempting to enter into the canyon.

"From any given point, the Indians can sit between the rocks and pick us off," the colonel says. "They can hold up in there for weeks, or until they run out of food or ammo."

Ranger Douglas and Stalking Wolf present a plan to the colonel.

"Let us climb over the hills and come up from behind their protected side. From that vantage point we should be able to secure the princess and end this once and for all."

The colonel agrees.

Stalking Wolf and Kenneth wait for night to fall. The full moon guides them over the sandstone rocks as they attempt to be as quiet as possible. The moon will also assist any lookouts that Isa-tai may have posted. There are no trees or bushes for cover; this land is desertlike, so they must use larger rocks for cover. Stalking Wolf slowly leads Kenneth up the small mountain and around the boulders. The night is still except for an occasional scream from a coyote.

A lookout has been posted, and Stalking Wolf signals for Kenneth to stop. He then removes his hunting knife from its sheath and places the blade into his mouth. He motions for Kenneth to remain at his location some twenty feet below him. Stalking Wolf slowly and meticulously maneuvers into attacking position. He lunges and grabs the unsuspecting Indian by placing his left hand over his mouth as he slits his neck and throat. The guard is gently laid to the ground. Stalking Wolf motions for Kenneth to join him.

They look down into the camp and see there is a large campfire, which is unusual for the circumstances. Men are seated around the fire—several white men and five Indians—eating and talking.

"Stalking Wolf, go back and tell Colonel Miles to send some troops up here, and we can end this now."

Stalking Wolf agrees and climbs back down the mountain. Kenneth studies the group and moves closer to get a look at the white men; one of them looks familiar. Slowly and steadily he moves closer, keeping an eye out for any lookouts. The sandstone rocks are much smaller on this side of the mountain and very slippery.

Hiding behind a medium-sized boulder, he looks at one of the cowboys, who is dressed in all black clothing and smoking a pipe. All of a sudden it hits him—Nathaniel Reed a.k.a. Texas Jack.

Texas Jack is wanted for robbing trains, banks, and some stagecoaches. This band of Comanche has now turned into a group of Comancheros. Kenneth looks around the camp, but there is no sign of Isa-tai or Falling Star.

Stalking Wolf arrives with about a dozen cavalry troopers.

They stop at the entrance to the hideout, and from a hundred yards away, Colonel Miles shouts out to the encampment, "This is the United States Army and the Texas Rangers. We have you surrounded. Give up or all of you will be shot down."

Texas Jack drops his pipe and reaches for his pistol. Kenneth takes aim and shoots the pistol out of his hand. The outlaw raises his hands in surrender as the others follow his lead.

The troopers cover the group as the remaining cavalry troopers ride in, unmolested. Texas Jack looks to Kenneth.

"You that boy deputy?"

Kenneth replies, "No, sir, I'm a Texas Ranger."

Stalking Wolf smiles.

They learn that Isa-tai took Falling Star and left the camp yesterday before the troopers arrived. They headed east with a group of five Indians. Kenneth and Stalking Wolf gather their horses and additional supplies. Stalking Wolf immediately begins tracking their path across the plateau, eastward.

Four days of hard riding and tracking have passed when Stalking Wolf suddenly holds up his right hand.

"Kenneth, they are very close. They cannot travel with Falling Star at this pace. She is slowing them down, and they know we are chasing them. The hoof prints from the horses are fresh—they are fully rounded in the ground, and the wind has not disturbed them."

"What do you suggest?"

Stalking Wolf is quiet for a moment.

"We must continue to follow them; however, we must also be weary of an ambush. They will stop and fight soon."

Eastward they continue with the dry, hot sun beating down on them, knowing that Falling Star is within reach. They, too, are fighting the elements of Mother Nature. The high Texas sun is sending down a heat that steals their energy. They can continue because their pack mule is loaded with water and supplies, things that Isa-tai does not have.

Another day passes, and Stalking Wolf once again holds up his hand.

"There, in the distance, I can see a small dust cloud from horses."

Kenneth removes his spyglass from a saddlebag.

"Yes, one, two, three—all seven are there. Six are walking their horses, and Falling Star is riding hers. They look exhausted. I do not see any supplies with them. I do not think that they can continue any more. Here—take a look."

Kenneth hands the spyglass to Stalking Wolf.

"I think that they will have to stop, and we can catch them then," he says as Stalking Wolf agrees.

"Yes, they will have to stop and rest. We can catch them at that point."

The sun sets on the western part of the plateau, and a small fire is seen in the not too far distance.

Stalking Wolf turns to Kenneth and says, "It is a signal to us to talk."

Kenneth looks at Stalking Wolf and replies, "Is it a trap or a peaceful signal?"

"I shall find out."

Stalking Wolf rides ahead. He announces himself and enters the camp, unknowing that Kenneth has followed and is a short distance away. Stalking Wolf dismounts his horses and places his right hand across his chest in a sign of friendship. Isa-tai returns the gesture.

"You are the scout of the white Ranger?"

"Yes, I ride with him."

The two stand in the middle of the camp while the other Indians have set down and are resting, totally exhausted from the chase. Falling Star is seated away from the others with a frightened look upon her face.

"We cannot go on; we are all exhausted and have no food or water. This Ranger, he will kill us and take the princess back."

At that moment, Kenneth walks his horse into the camp. The Indians jump from their resting place and reach for their guns as Kenneth shoots a rifle from the hands of one.

"No, Isa-tai, there has been enough killing," Kenneth says. "Can we talk peace?"

Isa-tai signals the others to drop their rifles. Kenneth dismounts his horse, and in a show of trustfulness, he places his pistol back into its holster. Isa-tai sits by the fire.

Kenneth says, "We have a supply mule with food and water for you; however, I ask that these hostilities end."

Isa-tai looks around his camp and into the faces of his remaining army and then asks, "What is to become of my people?"

Kenneth looks Isa-tai directly into his eyes.

"If we smoke the peace pipe here and now, I assure you that your people shall be granted land in what we call western Oklahoma and away from the Bureau of Indian Affairs. I have spoken to Colonel Mills, and he has guaranteed this will happen. You can hunt and fish without the interference from the white hunters."

Isa-tai looks back to Kenneth, and with a smile across his face, he removes his war paint and signals for Falling Star to sit next to Kenneth and Stalking Wolf. Her captivity has ended. They reach a peace agreement, and three days later, the nine of them ride into Fort Sill.

Colonel Mills is standing outside of his office.

"Just amazing," he says.

The five reporters standing there run to the telegraph office and send their stories:

"Texas Ranger Saves Indian Princess. Boy Deputy Turned Texas Ranger Has Entered into Indian Territory and Put an End to the Red River War; Brokers Peace Treaty."

Comanche Chief Parker is also at Fort Sill, waiting the return of his only daughter. Falling Star runs to her father and tells him of her adventure. Chief Parker nods his head to Ranger Douglas and Stalking Wolf in a show of appreciation.

The next morning, Chief Parker and the Indians are leaving and heading back to their reservation. He stops and leads a white stallion over to Kenneth.

"For saving my daughter and my people, I ask that you take this white stallion as a token of my appreciation and friendship."

Kenneth accepts the reins and moves his right hand over his chest. Chief Parker extends his hand toward Kenneth, and the two shake hands, a first for Chief Parker.

Kenneth, Stalking Wolf, and the eighteen-hand-tall white stallion Kenneth names Blanco head back to San Antonio.

"The newspapers are sure to beat us back, and I'll have more explaining to do to Marie."

She has plans of her own.

Chapter 13

Marie insists on an outdoor garden wedding, something she has read about in one of those eastern magazines. Mr. Yang, the Indians, and the five orphan children who have found a home at the Mission have all worked very hard in setting up the benches and chairs for what they think will be a small ceremony between the sixteen-year-old bride and her twenty-year-old groom. Weddings are common at their age at a time when Texas is young and growing also.

White benches and chairs are placed outside of the church facing west into the setting June sun. A center aisle leads to a white arbor covered in green vines and yellow roses. Cactus roses are spread throughout the garden setting, as if they know of the ceremony that is about to be performed, with their yellow flowers opened wide and smiling for all to see. Papier-mâché lights of all colors are strung across the entire setting. An altar awaits the couple at the end of the aisle with a table off to one side that is covered with a white cloth. Atop the table are two unity candles with a Calvary cross standing between them, as if shouting the words, "Faith based upon Hope based upon Love."

The wedding is larger than Rose, Father Ortega, and even Sheriff Chisholm can image. The eastern press has somehow received the news of the planned wedding between "The Boy Deputy of San Antonio" and his "Spanish Princess." Journalists from the East Coast and Europe are flooding into San Antonio. The East Coast and especially Europe have adopted the orphan boy turned lawman as their Wild West hero after his actions between the Chinese rail workers and the hired gunslingers just two years prior. They are starved for the latest news and happenings in his life.

News accounts of the wedding started to circulate in the eastern tabloids one month ago. "A Spanish Princess Has Captured the Heart of the Boy Deputy of San Antonio" as the daily headlines are nonstop.

"The Spanish Princess, Marie Garcia, was raised at the Mission of the Son in San Antonio and is the childhood sweetheart of our western hero. She teaches at the orphanage and also performs humanitarian work for the less fortunate in and around the San Antonio area, especially in Beanville.

The crowd of one hundred has grown into over one thousand. Photographers are setting up in the garden. Reporters are shoving their way past invited guest. The time has come as Kenneth and Father Ortega exit the church and walk to the altar. Kenneth is dressed in a white suit with a jacket that stops at his belt line. He has on a black bow tie and a ruffled white shirt. His yellow hair is brushed back and stops just above his collar. Mr. Yang had insisted on putting a shine on his boots that can reflect the smallest of lights, and they do. One of the orphans has begun to play music on the piano that has been moved from inside of the church to the other side of the altar.

Rose and Marie are inside of the church office finalizing their dresses. Neither knows who is the more nervous of the two: the mother who has prayed for this day since the two were children or the bride who has dreamed of this day for years.

Sheriff Chisholm knocks on the office door.

"It's time," is all he says.

Mother and daughter soon exit the office. Rose walks outside of the church and down the aisle and takes her place at the altar as her daughter's matron of honor. Sheriff Chisholm escorts Marie down the aisle to the march of "Here Comes the Bride." He is her unofficial stepdad and takes great pride in that responsibility. He thinks of the two as his kids. He takes his place next to Kenneth as his best man.

Marie is dressed in a solid white dress with a lace top, exposing a portion of her mocha-colored skin. The train is ten feet long, and two of the orphans assist her down the aisle as the guests all stand for her. On her left hand is a white corsage. Her veil is white and over her face as she approaches the altar. Her coal-black hair is pulled back into a bun atop the back of her head, as a smile beams from her, lighting up the entire ceremony.

Kenneth looks at this goddess that he is about to exchange vows with, and he thinks to himself, *God has blessed me this day.*

The San Antonio sun is setting atop the western hills and has cast an orange and yellow sky as far as one can see. The desert is silent as a western breeze sneaks upon the ceremony and with a gentle effort pushes the papier-mâché lights from side to side.

Father Ortega begins the ceremony with his heart full of so much joy and pride. He walks the two of them through their vows to one another, assisting them in the lighting of the unity candles, and he has one more duty to perform. He reaches down onto the table and under a cloth for an object that he had placed there just prior to the ceremony. He raises the object high into the air.

"I now pronounce you man and wife," he proclaims as he waves the Cross of Santo Domingo from side to side above their heads.

Kenneth and Marie stand and kiss to the sound of claps and cheers from the guests.

Onlookers soon slow their clapping and cheering once they recognize the cross. Could it be? How did the most precious treasure in all of Mexico end up here in San Antonio?

Kenneth and Marie do not notice or recognize the cross as something special, but they run down the aisle hand in hand, trying to avoid the corn and rice that is being thrown on them. Sheriff Chisholm has recognized the cross as have some of the reporters. Three of the reporters are running to their horses and ride off toward town, heading to the telegraph office more than likely.

Kenneth and Marie run to the front of the church, where Mr. Yang is waiting. The horse and buggy is ready to leave, and it is his honor to drive them to the rail station for their honeymoon trip to New Orleans. Mr. Yang looks upon his student and his wife as his kids also.

Rose is excited. Her daughter has married the man that she has loved since childhood, and her new son-in-law is now her son. Guests gather around the tables that are set up with food and drink. Sheriff Chisholm approaches Father Ortega as have numerous other guests, mostly eastern reporters.

The reporters begin shouting over the voices of the sheriff and others, asking questions about the cross:

"Father, is that the Cross of Santo Domingo, the cross that all of Mexico is looking for?"

"How did it get here, and why do you have it?"

Question after question soon echoes from the group of guests and reporters.

Father Ortega begins to explain.

"When I was in Mexico City, the bishop asked me to take the Cross to Texas and safeguard it so the Mexican government could not steal it. For the last twenty-seven years, the Cross has been here in San Antonio at the Mission of the Son. I feel comfortable now, knowing that San Antonio is a peaceful community and that the Cross will be safe from the thieves who are trying to destroy it. Also, this is a special day, so I used it in a ceremony uniting two souls as the Cross was meant to be used for."

New plans will have to be made for the safekeeping of the cross, for word will spread fast about the discovery of its location. There is no doubt in the mind of Father Ortega and Sheriff Chisholm that there will be many an outlaw heading to San Antonio for their fortune in gold.

Chapter 14

A year has passed, and a new one greets the young couple as Kenneth and Marie prepare for their customary early morning ride to see Mother Nature's offerings—he atop Blanco and she atop her gift from Stalking Wolf, a two-year-old Spanish mustang named Little Texas.

Rose stands on the porch of her home when the two wave good-bye to her as they leave the Mission and head out to their special place down by the river. The water's edge provides them with the opportunity to watch different creatures as they come to the river to fill their bellies with water.

He dismounts his horse and then spreads a blanket on the ground for her. He helps her dismount Little Texas and insists on carrying her to their newly made nesting place. They sit there, his arm around her shoulder, as she is snuggled next to her love.

"Kenneth, I need to tell you something, something very special."

He looks to his love, "Yes, mi amor?"

"In the spring, you shall become a father. Mother and I believe that a little girl is growing inside of me."

Kenneth is so excited he jumps from their nesting place with his arms reaching to the heavens.

"Thank you, Lord, thank you, Lord."

He stops and looks back to Marie. "Oh, my sweetheart, how can I help you?"

Marie is happy and smiles back to her husband.

"I think you have done enough."

She stands, and the two of them hug as if for the first time.

The Texas Rangers are kind to the young couple, allowing Kenneth to remain around San Antonio until the birth of his child. On May 1, Marie gives birth to a screaming baby girl.

"They are both doing well," Doc Wilson proclaims.

Marie is all smiles while lying in bed with her new baby girl wrapped in a blanket in her arms. Her husband, mother, Sheriff Chisholm, and Father Ortega are all standing in the room with her.

She looks over to Kenneth and says, "It is time for us to give our little darling her name."

"Liliana," he says, "after your mother, Rose Liliana Garcia."

A smile crosses their faces.

Kenneth loves being around San Antonio and playing with his daughter. There is no substitute for the smiles a child brings to her parents. The quality family time that he has spent with Marie and Liliana has filled his heart with much happiness and joy; however, Texas cannot stand still, and the Texas Rangers need their best as the dark cloud of violence is rumbling through the Wild West.

Chapter 15

Local law enforcement has curtailed the violence in San Antonio, but the smaller cattle towns are crying for assistance. The out-of-work cowboys have created a growing "hobo" population and will travel great distances for any type of work, either legal or not, and will often rustle cattle to make a living. These cowboys, who the eastern journalists say carry a trait of heroism, also have short fuses attached to volatile tempers. They ease their boredom with drink, tobacco, and cards.

The end of the Red River War has pretty much stopped the Indian aggression as the Comanche and Kiowa Tribes are now confined to their new home in western Oklahoma. Governor Lawrence Ross can now focus on more pressing issues, such as the three thousand desperados that now call Texas home.

The governor calls upon General Woodford Mabry, Major John Jones, Captain Junius Peak, and Captain Bill McDonald of the Texas Rangers to devise a plan to rid Texas of the outlaws. The three-year plan has two major components: first, the outlaw issue and any illegal activities; second, the Mexican and Indian marauders along the Rio Grande River.

General Mabry presents the plan to the governor.

"We need to divide Texas into districts," he says.

The general walks over to a map showing their plan.

"The Dallas/Fort Worth Squad will cover the north from the Indian Territory east to the Louisiana line and as far south as Waco. It is a large area; however, there are not many settlers west of Fort Worth. The Houston Squad will cover south of Tyler along the Louisiana line and along the Gulf of Mexico to Corpus Christi, and north to Waco.

The Austin Squad will cover central Texas. The San Antonio Squad will cover from Corpus Christi south along the Gulf of Mexico to Mexico and west to the King Cattle Ranch. El Paso and the southwest will be covered by—" The general hesitates and looks back to Major Jones, Captain Peak, and Captain McDonald.

"Yes, General. Please continue," the governor requests. "What about El Paso and our southwest?"

General Mabry takes a hard swallow, "Well, sir, Ranger Douglas shall cover the remaining area."

"What! How can one Ranger cover such a vast area full of outlaws, marauders, and that crazy Judge Roy Bean? Pecos County is a riot just waiting to happen."

The governor looks at his Ranger brain trust as if they have gone mad.

Captain McDonald stands from the table and says, "One riot—one Ranger."

The governor falls back into his chair, raising his arms and looking up to the ceiling as his arms fall to the chair rest.

"Look, gentlemen, I know that Ranger Douglas is a remarkable man, a hero to many and a legend to others, but I just cannot see sending him to his death. John Wesley Hardin is due to be released from prison soon. We all know that he will head straight to El Paso. Sheriff Chisholm and Father Ortega will string me up if we send Douglas out there. Not to say what his wife will do to me."

The governor looks over to Captain Peak and says, "You know, we told Marie three years ago that there would be no more gunfights—your words, Captain. Every time I go to San Antonio, I look in on the folks at the Mission, and she and her mother remind me of your words verbatim, Captain."

The Rangers all regather in a conference and discuss the matter; then, they present their decision to the governor: "Governor, we feel that Douglas and Stalking Wolf can do the job. Otherwise, we would not make such a recommendation."

The governor looks to each of his advisors as they nod in agreement.

"Well, gentlemen, may God have mercy on his soul and us for sending him into this hell's gate."

The Texas Rangers undergo the largest reorganization of their brief history. They are divided into four squads, and the bad news is hand delivered to Ranger Douglas and Stalking Wolf.

Captain McDonald arrives in San Antonio and visits his old friend, the sheriff.

Walking into the small office of the sheriff, Captain McDonald says in his husky, deep voice, "Billy Wayne, it has been too long."

Sheriff Chisholm extends a hand to his old army pal and says, "Yes, Bill, we should get together more often. You just don't know how much longer we will be around."

The two of them shake hands and laugh. They soon find chairs in the dust-covered office of the sheriff and take a seat.

"Well, Bill, what is it this time? You've not come all the way here without something important on your mind."

Captain McDonald removes his cowboy hat and looks straight into the eyes of his friend.

"Billy Wayne, I need your help and support."

Sheriff Chisholm looks to his old friend with a puzzled expression, knowing that he has always given McDonald his support and backing.

The two pull their chairs up to the only desk in the room as Captain McDonald explains the plan to his old friend, even including the expectation of John Wesley Hardin and his pending release from prison.

The sheriff mumbles to himself, "Hardin chasing Hardin."

"What did you say, Billy Wayne?"

"Oh, nothing—just thinking out loud. Well, my friend, shall we go out to the Mission together?"

Chapter 16

Fannie Porter's brothel has a reputation for attracting some of the most notorious outlaws, gunfighters, cowboys, and just about any desperado looking for a good time. On occasion, even lawmen can be seen frequenting the bordello, seeking the companionship of its young ladies.

Fannie was born in England and came to America with her parents when she was a small child. Her parents disappeared from her life, and Fannie found herself aboard a train bound for San Antonio.

She was adopted by a local merchant, but by the age of fifteen, she was working as a prostitute on the streets. A shrewd businesswoman and fast learner, she opened her own brothel by the time she reached the age of twenty.

Only girls between the ages of eighteen and twenty-five are hired to work in her brothel. She insists on her girls practicing clean and safe hygiene. Fannie's brothel gains fame for the cordial treatment given to its clients. No one ever sees one of her girls yelling from a balcony or hanging out in the street.

As she says to them, "Get your butt back inside, or I'll swat it with me broom."

Fannie advertises her place as a boarding home for young women housing five to eight ladies at any one time. From the exterior, her place looks no different than that of a general mercantile store with its faded gray wood siding. Once a customer passes through the double-door entrance, he enters into a world of elegance such as he has likely never seen before.

Stepping into the foyer, your eyes fix on the first sight—a giant, sparkling crystal chandelier that is hanging from the twenty-four-foot ceiling, just ten feet inside of the doorway. Each step you take sinks into the plush, crushed red-velvet carpet that runs from one wall to the other.

Gazing around the foyer, you have three paths to choose from. Straight in front of you is an oak staircase looking as if a fresh coat of varnish has just been applied to it because you can actually see your reflection staring back at you. At the top of the stairs is Heaven's Gate, or so it is called. The ladies' private rooms are located to either side.

"Come on, my darling" is Fannie's usual enticement. "You will love my little ladies."

Fannie is always the marketer, making sure that she speaks with every customer as he enters her establishment.

A parlor is to the right, and a lounge is to the left with a large, oak archway protecting the entrance to each. An oak chair rail runs along the walls of each room, separating the oak slats that run down from the ceiling and the imported cherry-red wall dressing that anchors the walls.

Fannie furnishes her place with the finest leather sofas and chairs that money can buy. In the lounge there are oak tables laced with red leather inserts. The bar is made of stained oak wood with imported brass accents, and behind the bar is a mirror with beveled edges that runs the entire length of the wall from one side to the other. There is always a scent of honeysuckle in the air that is so strong it intoxicates your senses. Fannie also makes it a point to serve chilled champagne to her best customers.

She does not care much for lawmen, although William Pinkerton of the Pinkerton Detective Agency is a regular visitor. Pinkerton is well-known by the San Antonio jailers for bringing to justice several thieves while working for the railroad system.

This day, he has to bail Fannie out of jail for vagrancy (the legal euphemism used to charge women for prostitution). He and Fannie are leaving the jail when they are met at the entrance by a tall man wearing a gray long-sleeve shirt and a white cowboy hat. Attached to the left side of the man's chest is a five-point star encircled by a silver ring. William Pinkerton introduces Fannie to Texas Ranger Kenneth Douglas.

"Oh, my dear, Bill—it's him." They had met once before when she was fifteen and he was just a young deputy.

Fannie's eyes nearly pop out of her head when she sees this man. Finding it hard to breathe, she cannot speak as she feels her heart pounding rapidly as if it were about to explode. She glances up to him as he tips his hat to her, with those piercing blue eyes looking straight into her soul, just like that day years ago.

"Bill, he saved my life when I was young."

William Pinkerton glances down at her and with an astonished look upon his face and says, "Saved your life? What are you talking about?"

"The Chinese Lunar Year Parade—I was the prostitute taken hostage that day."

"That was you? That story hit every English-speaking newspaper across the country and in Europe."

"Yes, I have tried to thank him numerous times. I have even talked with his wife. She tells me that he is a peaceful man and does not seek the glory or attention that his heroism has placed upon him."

Pinkerton helps her back to the brothel because she is so starstruck, having just met her hero. She is a regular subscriber to the New York and Boston newspapers. She has them shipped to San Antonio along with just about every other periodical that documents the adventures of the Texas Ranger. She cannot read enough about her hero. She has even traveled to New York City to see the Broadway play, *Texas Ranger*. There are more stories written about him than all of the other Texas lawmen combined, but he has never gave a single interview or commented on any of the stories—just not his way.

Fannie has hired a young lady by the name of Annie Rogers, who brings her friend Etta Place to the brothel as well. Their outlaw boyfriends often visit them whenever they are in the San Antonio area. Kid Curry and Annie Rogers as well as Etta Place and the Sundance Kid are quite the items when they manage to get together. Kid and Sundance often come to San Antonio to see their girlfriends and will leave just as word starts spreading throughout the town that they are there. They are members of the Wild Bunch Gang.

The Wild Bunch is not wanted in Texas; however, they are well-known for their daring train robberies in Nevada and Montana. Part of the Hole in the Wall Gang, the leader of this Wild Bunch Gang, Butch Cassidy, also knows of the reputation that precedes Ranger Douglas; and he takes it very seriously. He believes Douglas's deeds are not like some dime-novel cowboy propaganda that the others speak of.

One day, word soon spreads throughout San Antonio that Kid Curry and his brother are in town. The sheriff is worried, because they walk around town in broad daylight, in and out of the hotels and saloons, and seem in no hurry to leave. He also knows that if they stay very long, Sundance and Butch are probably not far behind them.

Sheriff Ed Farr of Wyoming has supplied Chisholm with the detailed information that he needs on this bunch. Robert Leroy Parker, better known as Butch Cassidy, is the leader. Members of the gang are his best friend, Elzy Lay, Harry A. Longabaugh alias the Sundance Kid, the Tall Texan, Kid Curry, "Flat-Nose" George Curry, Bob Meeks, Sam Ketchum, Will Carver, Camila Hanks, and Laura Bullion.

Rumors have spread in Wilcox, Wyoming, that the gang is headed to San Antonio for something big. A waitress at the Harvey House restaurant there had overheard Butch Cassidy and the Tall Texan in an argument over control of the gang. She told Sheriff Farr that Cassidy wants to head to Texas for a big haul. The Tall Texan wanted the gang to head to gold country in California. The threat of Sundance's gun settled that argument.

Sheriff Chisholm is standing outside his office, sipping on a cup of coffee as he sees Ben Kilpatrick, alias the Tall Texan, and Will Carver, alias News Carver, ride into town and straight to the Menger Hotel.

The sheriff takes a seat in his rocker just outside his office and takes another sip of his coffee as he wonders, *What are they doing in San Antonio in the middle of the week, a Wednesday?*

They are not covered with travel dust, the gray dirt that covers a person when he has been exposed to long hours on the trail. They are clean shaven and do not carry any travel bags with them, which causes the sheriff's suspicion to grow even greater. One by one, the gang is showing up at the Menger Hotel.

What are they up to? the sheriff thinks. *There is no large cash or payroll here; could they just be hiding from the Utah, Wyoming, and Nevada lawmen? What big "haul" is Cassidy after? I'll just have to put extra deputies on this weekend.*

The sheriff checks his list that Sheriff Farr has supplied: Butch Cassidy—check; the Sundance Kid—check; the Curry brothers—check; the Tall Texan—check. One by one, all are checked off of the list except for Sam Ketchum.

Where the hell is Ketchum? He is the native Texan. No family or relatives. I don't like this. Well, a few more days, and Kenneth and Stalking Wolf should be back.

Sam Ketchum is the outcast of the group, a native Texan who has spent the majority of his adult life either in jail or along the Mexican border. He has also spent time with several of the border gangs that includes the Buscanerio, the Mexican Indian outlaws. The Buscanerio are infamous for their association with the Rurales under Mexican President Diaz. They are more murderous than any civilized outlaw has ever thought of being. They kill women and children more for sport than any other possible reason.

The sheriff goes back into his office and reviews his lists of all of the standby deputies. He sends a deputy to advise each of them to be prepared on Friday and over the weekend just in case this crazy bunch tries something stupid.

Chapter 17

This is a great Saturday. Kenneth and Stalking Wolf are back from another assignment, and Marie is very excited as she and her husband start out on their customary early morning ride to see Mother Nature's newest blessing. This was a regular event they started when they first fell in love, and they have continued treating each ride as a new honeymoon. Their love for each other has grown with each passing day, bringing them together as one. His thoughts are always of her and Liliana, and her thoughts are always of him and Liliana.

Liliana is now five years old and reminds them so much of Marie when she was her age, with her long black hair to her shoulders, her big brown eyes, and that smile that can light up your heart every time you see her. Her missing two front teeth are courtesy of Mr. Yang. He was pushing her on the rope swing that he and Sheriff Chisholm had made for the kids and attached it to that lone oak tree in the court yard, when she went flying.

Grandfather and Stalking Wolf are leaving with their families at the same time to head into the farmers' market, while Father Ortega and Rose are leaving with the remaining orphans and are heading into town. That leaves Mr. Yang and Sheriff Chisholm fighting for attention from Liliana.

Marie yells back to them, "Do not push her on that swing while we are gone."

They all laugh and smile as each group goes their separate way.

In the distance is a cowboy watching their every move from a spyglass. Next to him, waiting intently, is a Buscanerio. One mile away from them and hidden from sight of the Mission and away from any path that may be taken is the Hole in the Wall Gang, the Wild Bunch along with five additional Buscanerio Indians, and several other outlaws. They have scouted the Mission and have studied the trails that Kenneth and Marie take when leaving the Mission.

They wait for the last wagon to leave, and then they start a slow ride toward the Mission. After thirty minutes, they spank their horses into a fast gallop, and just like a swarm of locusts, they stampede into the Mission courtyard. Immediately, they draw their guns and open fire on Sheriff Chisholm, sending him to the ground in a hail of bullets. Mr. Yang grabs Liliana and starts running toward the barn, but they are targeted, and he falls to the ground still holding her in his arms—neither one of them reach safety.

These warriors of the devil posted no lookouts and have no knowledge that Kenneth and Marie have returned from their ride and are in the barn. Hearing the gunshots, Kenneth runs from the barn with his pistol drawn, and he sees Mr. Yang and Liliana fall to their deaths. He is able to fire two shots and sends two of these desperados back to hell, along the path from which they came, but he is shot in the right shoulder and the right temple and falls to the ground unconscious.

Marie sees the love of her life fall just steps from her. He is lying there unconscious and feared dead. She summons courage from deep within her soul and kneels by her husband's side. She takes his pistol in her hand, and she puts the four remaining bullets into these villains, sending them back to hell with their companions.

Two riders approach and empty their guns into her as she kneels there. She falls atop her husband.

Stalking Wolf, Grandfather, and their families are the first to return and see the devastation that has fallen upon the Mission. Grandfather leads the wagons away as Stalking Wolf enters the courtyard. By the lone oak tree lies Sheriff Chisholm, his pistol still in its holster. Twenty feet from him is Mr. Yang lying facedown and Liliana lying face up, both of their bodies riddled with bullets. Outside of the barn is Kenneth facedown in the dirt with Marie lying across his back. Scattered throughout the courtyard are six other dead bodies, two that look like Buscanerio Indians and four cowboys.

A slight moan comes from Kenneth as Stalking Wolf rushes to his partner. He is alive, but he is the only one. The Indian lifts Kenneth up as Father Ortega, Rose, and the others enter the courtyard. Shock and terror has taken over their thoughts as the orphans are led away from this disaster.

Rose cannot control herself as she sees her daughter and her granddaughter lifeless. Father Ortega attempts to comfort her, but this tragedy has already taken hold of her. Kenneth is taken into one of the nearby houses as Stalking Wolf attempts to render aid to his partner.

Two weeks pass, and Stalking Wolf has stayed by the side of his partner. Doc Wilson has tended to the lawman as best he can. A small cemetery with four headstones has found a home under that lone oak tree. Three Franciscan monks have arrived from a mission in El Paso and are attending to the orphans and to the church business during this time of crisis.

Grandfather, a *diyin* (shaman) and an Apache practitioner of religion has been there as well. He is performing the Life Giver ceremony. The four hoops—black for the eastern wind, blue for the southern wind, yellow for the western wind, and white for the northern wind—have all been placed onto the ground by a bonfire. An eagle feather is attached to the four sides of each hoop, giving strength to that hoop and to Kenneth. Grandfather raises his hands high into the air as the other Apache chant to the Life Giver. A young Indian boy bangs a drum to a steady beat: *boom, boom, boom.*

"Can you hear me, Life Giver?" they all chant.

The curing ceremony has continued nonstop since the Day of the Devil.

Father Ortega does not care for this ancient religious ceremony, but with two weeks of no movement from Kenneth, Rose is ready to try anything to bring her son back to her.

As the sun is setting on the fifteenth day, Kenneth opens his left eye. Stalking Wolf is kneeling at the end of the bed and praying. Rose is seated in a nearby rocking chair, praying along with Father Ortega. He turns his head and sees Rose as her eyes meets his. She leaps from her resting place and runs over to him, just like that day at the Morris farm. Father Ortega and Stalking Wolf soon join her.

Chapter 18

A month has passed since that day, and Kenneth is now up and moving around, fully recovered from his wounds. All that remains is a scar that runs from his right eye back to his hairline. He has talked with Stalking Wolf and Father Ortega about what has happened as best as his memory will allow him. Father Ortega has said that they stole the Cross of Santo Domingo. He blames himself for not sending the Cross to a safe haven as Sheriff Chisholm had suggested.

Kenneth and Rose visit the cemetery together daily. They place yellow roses on each grave, signs of a happier time. They carry heavy hearts. That blank stare that he had as a young boy has returned and taken over his face. Friends gather and offer their condolences, but he sees no one; he hears no one. They speak to him, but he hears no sounds. His heart has been ripped from his chest. His will has been taken. He shall continue to breathe, to live, but only as a hardened shell of the man that he once was.

At the end of each day, Kenneth walks to the west side of the church and watches the setting sun as it spreads its colorful show across the heavens the way it did that special day six years ago. Isolation and depression have entered into his mind, bringing insecurity and a dark cloud of hopelessness with it.

He wonders, *Shall I seek revenge? No, that is not God's way. Revenge will only tarnish the memory of my family.*

I can only pray for the future and remember the past—her hand holding mine, my hand holding hers, her breath upon me as we lay together as one. I remember the sacrifices that each of us made for the other, now knowing that her soul is in a distant place with our daughter. Their spirits are here with me.

The heavens cry this day, another day of darkness that has captured my world. My heart is heavy with the loneliness that the Day of the Devil has brought, for they are in the hands of the Lord, in a place far away from me. The tears that are falling from the angels are racing toward this earth, a place that I no longer share with them.

There is nothing harder than the empty feeling inside of one's soul with the loss of a companion and a child. Two lives taken in a senseless act of violence and greed—a child's life taken as it has only begun; a mother's life taken while attempting to protect her loved ones.

There is no explanation as to why people act the way that they do. Their needs and their greed are elevated to a level of importance to them, that the taking of human life is meaningless to their greed; in their mind.

How does one with no heart and a lost soul move on? How do I live, breathe, or survive from one day to the next. Some people go through life as if their world is the only existence that God has made on this earth. A lost heart that has been ripped from the very soul of a person, a soul that cannot hear the singing of the birds; a soul that cannot enjoy the love that God's creatures offer to him. I cannot cry, for I do not see sadness. I cannot see life at all. I can end my suffering, for that is my fate and a curse that has been laid at my feet.

Kenneth removes his pistol from its holster, and as he holds it in his left hand, he starts spinning the cylinder with his thumb.

Is it a selfish act to leave my body here on this earth so that my spirit may join that of my wife and my daughter? I hear their calls. I see their arms reaching for me. Shall God condemn my soul here while my spirit walks with theirs? Shall I ...

Stalking Wolf reaches to his partner and slaps him across the side of his head. He will not let his partner drown himself in self-pity. He has asked Grandfather to perform another Apache ritual, the Spirit Healer. Apaches believe that when a person, animal, or plant has stopped living, their spirit continues. For the Apache, the animal gives up its body; however, the spirit continues on this earth. The Spirit Healer is a ceremony to keep the living and the dead spirits separated. A ceremony that requires large explosions and drums pounding as the women all dance while raising their hands to the heavens and then falling to the earth as if they have entered into another dimension. Large bonfires light up the night sky and expose the shadows of these spirits.

Grandfather performs the ceremony as ashes from the fire are racing toward heaven. He takes a deep breath and blows the smoke of security upon Kenneth's face. He then places the mask of disguise upon him. Kenneth must wear this mask for a period of three years to hide his face from the spirits of the dead. He cannot take it off in the presence of any living person, and he must wear the mask of disguise at all times during the day and especially at night throughout the entire three-year period.

The next week, Kenneth and Stalking Wolf receive a telegram from the Texas Rangers headquarters in Austin detailing new orders. Their mission is to seek out and bring to justice the remaining members of the Hole in the Wall Gang, the Wild Bunch, and any Buscanerio Indian that may be riding with them. The Pinkerton Agency is currently chasing Butch and Sundance; however, the others are running across southwest Texas.

They mount their horses, Kenneth atop Blanco and Stalking Wolf atop his new painted Spanish mustang, and they leave the courtyard. Everyone has come out to wish them farewell on their new adventure: Grandfather and his Apache family, the monks with the orphans, Father Ortega with Rose. She stands there fighting the tears of sorrow, not knowing if she will ever see her only living family member again.

As the two of them ride west into the setting sun, Rose is comforted by the last words that she heard from Stalking Wolf: *As long as I am alive, the Ranger shall never ride alone.*

PART TWO
CUBA

A Continuation of Charles Santana's Account

Chapter 19

Adventures have been recorded, and stories have been written of the masked man and his Lipan Apache Indian partner as they saved lives and brought justice to Texas. A legend has spread across this nation about a hero created by the eastern and European journalists, which is attention that Kenneth did not want or care for. Time has passed, but he still carries a heavy heart for a soul mate and daughter who were taken from him, robbing him of the love that he may never know again and the smiles that a child brings to a parent each day.

Now, a call to glory is sweeping across this great land—a call for help from a small island whose people dream of the freedoms that are enjoyed by a people just ninety miles away. An American army is being assembled to answer this call to glory. The Indian Wars have left many a soldier on the battlefield, and the American Civil War continues to haunt this nation. Soldiers and warriors are needed to fill these depleted ranks.

These calls for help have rung out across Texas and into Old Mexico. The Ranger and his partner are ready and willing to help. Captain "Wild Bill" MacDonald has sent them on many journeys in the name of justice and fair play; however, he has one more mission for the Ranger. This is a mission that he must tackle alone, for his aging partner has another calling that he must answer.

Volunteers are being assembled, and the Texas Rangers have been called upon for help. Specifically, Ranger Douglas is to report to the First United States Volunteer Cavalry Regiment in San Antonio.

Chapter 20

The USS *Maine* arrived in Havana Bay unannounced on a courtesy visit and remained there to protect the life and belongings of the Americans in Cuba. The ship exploded and sank on February 15, 1898.

The "yellow press," a term given to biased American newspapers, called for immediate military action.

The Spanish-American War is officially just a few months into its existence when Assistant Secretary of the Navy Theodore Roosevelt and his long-time friend Doctor Leonard Wood approach the Department of War with the idea of establishing a military cavalry regiment of volunteers to assist Cuba in its fight for independence from Spanish rule. The war is being fought on two basic fronts: one in Cuba and the second in the Philippines.

Under pressure from President William McKinley, the Department of War grants Wood and Roosevelt's request—with stipulations, of course.

Leonard Wood, an army doctor and Congressional Medal of Honor recipient for his accomplishments during the Indian Wars of the 1880s, will be colonel. He is the highest ranking officer of the regiment and in command of all of the activities. Theodore Roosevelt, who has no military experience, will be lieutenant colonel.

The Department of War makes one finial stipulation. They call upon one of their finest and bravest soldiers, Captain Anthony Salvatory. He is a veteran of the Indian Wars, and his reputation as a leader and organizer has received the attention of many top-ranking military officials in Washington. Captain Salvatory is assigned as an advisor to both men; however, Washington looks at his assignment more as an insurance policy in case the regiment is placed in an horrific situation.

Chapter 21

May 1898—San Antonio, Texas

Colonel Wood and Lieutenant Colonel Roosevelt meet Captain Salvatory in San Antonio. They set up camp on the southwest side of the city at an old Spanish church, the Mission of the Son, which is in a centrally located area with weather somewhat like that of Cuba, hot and humid. The First United States Volunteer Cavalry Regiment is now recruiting volunteers. They will come from Arizona, New Mexico, Old Mexico, Indian Territory, and right here in Texas.

The recruiters seek men who, with little or no training, can be ready to the fight the Spanish soldiers in Cuba. They want men who can ride fast and shoot straight! What they get are out-of-work cowboys (myself included), Indians, outlaws, and some men from the East, who think of this venture as a sporting match. It is obvious to us that Lieutenant Colonel Roosevelt—"Teddy" as he wants us to call him—is running the show. Heck, we would follow him into hell if he just asks us to. Looking back today, I think we did.

Teddy now has his regiment, 1,250 strong, but he wants one more person. He wants the man that he has read about in newspaper accounts and magazine articles. He wants the man whose adventures throughout Texas have spawned numerous dime-novel periodicals. He wants the man who has fought the Indians and then brokered a peace treaty with them. He wants the man who has taken the outlaw out of Texas. He wants the man who brought security to the Mexican immigrants, the cattle ranchers, and the farmers. He wants a God-fearing man; he wants Texas Ranger Kenneth Douglas.

Chapter 22

Starting out as a small Spanish mission some one hundred years earlier, the Mission of the Son has developed into a self-supporting rancho that houses seventy-five orphans. The grounds consist of the original church building and bell tower, a pole barn, sleeping quarters for the orphans, a schoolhouse, a galley building, a dairy barn, a dozen small houses, and numerous other buildings.

The Mission has become the center of activity for southwest San Antonio, with just about every farm animal that you can imagine from pigs to chickens. The vegetable farm raises crops to feed the Mission, and the extras go to the local farmers' market. It is obvious to us why Teddy chose this location to set up training camp.

The newest additions to the compound are the horse barn, corral, and paddock. There are eight Mexican families and two Lipan Apache Indian families living and working at the Mission. The Mexican families take care of the farm animals and the crops, while the Apache are busy capturing and breaking wild Spanish mustangs for a new military contract that has been awarded to the Mission.

The three monks who are assigned to the Mission live in one of the houses, and their main responsibility is the care and education of the orphans and any other child seeking a Catholic education. They run a taut ship, as I learn in Sunday school. The wooden ruler is their weapon of choice, and across the knuckles of your hand is their favorite target.

The oldest and original home is that of Rose Garcia. She and her family came to the Mission nearly twenty-five years ago. I do not know all of her story, but she is related to the Ranger—I just do not know how. She is in charge of the galley and is Father Ortega's confidant and assistant. My parents and the other families look at her as a saint; she always goes out of her way to help others.

Chapter 23

This day finds the Mission full of activity. Everyone is extremely busy with their daily chores; however, this is a special day. Buildings are being painted, and all of the furniture is being cleaned. The grounds are being spruced up to look as good as humanly possible, for they are expecting a visit from a special person.

Our canvas military tents are set up just to the west of the horse stables. A First United States Volunteer Cavalry Regiment flag flies high in the center of our compound, yet none of us in the regiment is the special guest who has everyone so excited. They are expecting him to return any day and at any time.

The Texas sun has a way of draining all of your energy right out of you, especially when it is high in the cloudless sky and beating directly down on you. The activity in the Mission grounds all but stops, and we are allowed to take a break from killing the hay bales when two riders approach and enter through the main gate to the Mission.

A solid-white stallion, eighteen hands high, and a painted mustang next to it pass under the oval archway leading into the main courtyard. Everyone's attention is immediately drawn to the two riders, one a Lipan Apache Indian and the other a white man atop the stallion. All of the children have stopped playing and are standing in the yard watching as the two riders slowly enter. The Indians have stopped their horse whispering techniques, and all of us are moving toward the fence that separates the Mission from us.

The rider of the stallion sits high in the black saddle, holding both reins in his right hand with his white cowboy hat pulled down attempting to fight off the bright Texas sun. His shoulders are square and his head is held high. He is wearing *chaparajos* (chaps), leather britches or wraparound leggings to protect his legs, a full-length duster for protection from the sun, and equestrian black boots that stop just short of his knees. The duster is open and pulled back to expose a Colt .45, a Texas six-shooter, which is snuggled in its black holster hanging from the rider's left hip. The bottom of the holster is tied to the rider's leg, just like that of a gunfighter. At the top of the holster is a five-pointed silver star enclosed inside a silver circle: a Texas Ranger's badge.

The Indian is dressed in buckskin leather pants with a breechcloth and a flannel shirt. He is wearing leather boots that are rolled down just below his knees. Across his forehead is a wide cloth headband, a standard piece of clothing of the Lipan Apache. He looks like an old army scout from years past, a confident man riding next to his partner.

The entire compound of men, women, children, and even us watch intently as these two slowly walk their horses onto the Mission grounds and straight to the small cemetery. No one can speak a word, as there is a chill running up and down our spines. I cannot believe that it is really him, that he really exists.

Not a single time has he looked around the compound; he just stares at the cemetery, his eyes are fixed upon the four headstones. They stop their horses at the gate entrance to the cemetery, and he dismounts by throwing his left leg over the rear of his horse, keeping his weapon exposed and at the ready—a sign of experience. Every eye in the compound is on the two of them as he removes his duster and throws it across the saddle. He removes an object from one of the saddlebags. I cannot tell what it was, only that it is wrapped in a cloth. The Indian grabs the reins to the beautiful white creature and walks the two horses toward the barn.

I study him as he stands there outside of the cemetery in his long-sleeve tan shirt with that bright Texas Ranger badge attached to his left chest and the shining spurs attached to his riding boots.

Heck, he scares me just looking at him.

I watch as he walks into the cemetery and kneels in front of two of the headstones. The four of them are lined up in a row as if standing at attention. He removes his hat, and his long blond hair falls down to his shoulders. He cups his hands and says a prayer. He then performs the Holy Trinity, picks up that object that he has wrapped in a cloth, and stands up. He turns and faces the compound. I feel as if those bright blue eyes of his are piercing right through me.

Two of the orphan boys who are standing outside of the church take off, running inside as fast as their little legs can carry them.

"Father! Father!" Their voices echo down the hallway.

Captain Salvatory throws his cigarette to the ground and immediately goes inside the command tent and tells Roosevelt, "Teddy, our man has arrived."

Lieutenant Colonel Roosevelt, who is seated at a makeshift desk, stops his writing and looks up to the captain and says, "This is a good day, Captain" as a feeling of uneasiness begins to creep into the back of his mind.

Father Ortega and Rose are in the office, which is located at the rear of the church building, when they hear the two boys running and screaming down the aisle.

"Father, he is here!" the oldest forces from his body.

"Father, Texas Ranger Douglas is here. I know it is him," the younger one says as he gasps for a breath. "Father, he is riding the white horse, just like you said he would."

Father Ortega turns to Rose and says with a big smile, "Our boy has come home."

Rose runs past the two boys and Father Ortega as fast as she can, up the aisle, and out the church door, stopping on the porch looking for him.

She is followed closely by Father Ortega and their two messengers. Both of her hands cover her mouth as she sees him standing there in the courtyard. Those tears of joy that had vanished from her have returned. She runs posthaste across the yard as quick as her aged legs will carry her, with Father Ortega not far behind her.

"Kenneth! Kenneth!" she cries with her arms outstretched, reaching for him. As they come together, he hugs the only parents he has ever known.

Chapter 24

Where the hell is Glenn Nagle? He knows that reveille is at 0600 hours. He's the bugler for this regiment, and he is not here. Sergeant Martin will have my head if he is not—wait a minute. Nagle is not here in our tent and neither is Cole Scudder or Eric Bade. I hope they did not go into town to that Mexican cantina again. Sarge will have my butt if I cannot find them.

The sound of wagons rolling into the Mission draws my attention away from our truants and toward the courtyard. There are two lines of wagons, one appears to be local ranchers and farmers bringing in supplies for the big shindig that is planned for Ranger Douglas, and the others appear to be—yes, it is supplies for us. I can see Fort Sam Houston stamped on the side of the wagons. I hope that they are bringing those new Krag-Jørgenson carbine rifles for us.

Well, look there. I don't believe it, Sergeant Martin is leading a wagon full of my tentmates. Obviously, I was right, and they did go into town last night.

Sarge looks directly at me.

"Charlie, give me a hand with these three. There is no reveille today. We are receiving supplies from Fort Sam Houston, as well as those new Krag rifles that fire smokeless powder. We are also getting some of those new Colt automatic-firing machine guns along with a couple of dynamite guns that are also on their way."

I walked over to the wagon and looked at my so-called friends, all three of whom are passed out cold to the world. Nagle is snoring so loud that he could wake the dead; Bade is fast asleep with a smile on his face as if he were still chasing the Mexican girls down at the cantina; and

Scudder is stretched out in the back of the wagon with the only sound coming from him is ongoing flatulence.

We get all three of them unloaded and into our tent before the captain can see us or them and before we are ordered to head over to the supply wagons to help with the unloading.

"Sarge, I don't think that there are enough rifles here for everyone."

Sarge looks at me with a puzzled expression.

"Well," he says, "some of our guys will just have to use their own Winchester rifles and pistols then."

It is around 7:00 AM when I see Ranger Douglas walk out of Miss Rose's house and over to the command tent. He must have been in there an hour before Colonel Wood and Captain Salvatory walk out. I see the colonel and captain talking outside of the tent for a couple of minutes, and then the captain heads over to the stables and Colonel Wood walks over to the supply area. They seem happy; both have smiles on their faces and are laughing loudly.

∗   ∗   ∗   ∗

"Kenneth, I need your help on a personal matter," Teddy says. "I asked you to remain here inside the tent so that I could speak to you in private, because I do not want anyone else to hear this. I have never been in battle before. I have never killed another human, much less even shot at a man before. Heck, the only time I have ever even fired a rifle was at some wild game on a hunting expedition in the Dakotas. If you agree to this appointment that President McKinley is offering, you must leave for Cuba in a week. I need you to train me how to ride fast and shoot straight, please! Now I do not know of the tragedy that fell upon you and your family, nor do I pretend to understand what runs through a man's mind after suffering such a tragedy. But let me assure you of this: if you accept this congressional appointment and this presidential assignment as a captain in the United States Army and as a special agent for the president, I will do everything in my power to see that you return safely back home. I promise this to you in the name of God and on my dead wife's grave."

He slams his right fist down upon the table.

Then in a soft voice Roosevelt says to Kenneth, "Son, there comes a time in a man's life when destiny takes over whether he wants it to or not. That path is controlled by God, and he has decided on your path before you were born. Don't give me an answer now. Go and talk it over with Father Ortega and Miss Garcia. I'll see you tonight at the barbeque."

*   *   *   *

Kenneth leaves the command tent and stops off at the corral. I watch as he talks with Stalking Wolf and some of the other Apache. I see Stalking Wolf place his hand on Douglas's shoulder and say something to him.

I am still standing by the supply wagons, watching Ranger Douglas, when all of a sudden I hear Sarge yelling again, "Santana, are you going to help us unload these wagons or are you going to day dream the entire day?"

"Sorry, Sarge."

It takes us all morning and most of the afternoon to get all of those wagons unloaded, about the time the three musketeers join us.

"Well, you ladies finally got around to helping us?"

Sarge pulls no punches on anyone.

I watch Ranger Douglas most of the day; there is just something special about him that draws the attention of all of us. He spends most of the day with the orphans, just as if he were one of them. As the day is ending, he and Father Ortega walk through the complex, talking to the kids and some of us. I feel privileged just listening to him speak. I am impressed with the way he cares for the kids and the respect he shows toward us, toward everyone.

They walk over to the back of the Mission, watching that infamous sunset.

*   *   *   *

Father Ortega looks over to his son and says, "I'm retiring—Mexico City is sending another priest. Rose is with the cancer; she does not want you to know. She wishes for you to continue your work, and in time she will speak with you. Kenneth, I will take care of your mother."

The look of shock soon spreads over Kenneth's face.

"Father, I should stay and help with her care. Stalking Wolf must leave the Rangers and care for his people. I have met with many accomplishments, many tragedies, and so many heartbreaks. The time has come for me to …"

Father Ortega interrupts, "Kenneth, God has laid out a plan for you, a destiny. You have been chosen to help his people. Many callings will scream across this land for you. He will guide you through many more adventures. That is your calling; that is your destiny."

Kenneth stands there as his head slowly rises from his chest and meets the eyes of his father.

"I understand that the needs of the many outweigh and overshadow my needs, my desires, and my wishes. If this is the path that God has laid out for me, then so it shall be. I shall answer this call from a people in another land. I shall speak with Colonel Roosevelt about his cavalry regiment."

Father Ortega leans forward, hugs his son, and says, "Kenneth, I need to tell you something. It's a story that I promised would remain with me, a story about you and how you came to be with us. I promised my best friend that this information would never find you; however, with his death, I believe that I am relieved of that obligation. More than that, I truly believe that knowing your youthful history will help you understand why I believe that you are God's chosen one."

Kenneth stares back at Father Ortega and replies, "Father, please. Chosen one?"

Father Ortega continues, "What I mean by chosen one is that many of his people struggle to be safe and secure from the evil that is spread by the devil. All creatures great and small need a certain level of security in their life. Man needs to know that he has the ability to safely provide for his family. You might be that safety blanket that is spread out so people can meet their obligations and the needs of their family to prosper, to grow."

"Well, Father, I guess there is a need for men to volunteer to help others, but …"

Once again, Father Ortega interrupts, "Kenneth, you are aware that you are an orphan. We have had many discussions about that; however, I have always kept the whole story, the truth from you."

Father Ortega takes Kenneth by the arm as they walk away from the Mission and toward the desert.

"When you were just two and a half years old, you arrived in San Antonio aboard the first Orphan Train. You were the youngest and last orphan to be led out onto that stage. I remember it just as if it were yesterday. Sheriff Chisholm saw something special in a dust-covered, towheaded little boy that day, and as the others were leaving the room, he gave me the two dollars so that you could be placed with the Mission."

Kenneth stands there with his eyes wide open and his attention on each word.

"Your birth name is Kenneth Douglas Hardin. You were born in New York City. I have attempted to contact your mother and your siblings over the years, but after numerous attempts, I have failed. I believe that your five brothers and sisters were sent along the same path as you. Rose does not know of this, only you and I. Your destiny was laid out long before today.

"So, my son, when I say that God has chosen you to protect his people from evil, I mean there will be many callings from many different lands. Should your destiny lead you to Cuba or some other foreign land—that is your destiny."

Kenneth says with an astonished look on his face, "But, Father, what about Rose? She is the only mother I have ever known. The two of you have been—you are—my parents. How can I leave knowing that in a short time she will leave this world?"

A small smile sneaks onto the face of Father Ortega.

"We all shall be called to heaven some time. We do not know when. That is God's decision. Rose will talk to you in time. She is finally at peace after the Day of the Devil. I will be at her side every day until she joins Marie and Liliana. She is my responsibility, and I owe her that. I promise you this."

"Father, do you think that I should accept the offer from the president and Colonel Roosevelt?"

"I think that you can only ask God that question and follow his advice. I am just saying that Rose and I will be fine and for you not to worry about either of us."

The two of them stand together as the moon has chased the sun from the sky—the old man full of wisdom and the young man seeking his knowledge and his advice.

As Father Ortega returns to the gathering in the courtyard, Kenneth walks away with his mind wondering.

Is this what I must do—travel to another land to fight some foe who I do not know, to help free a people so that they can live in peace, so they can prosper and their families grow? Must people die so that others may live?

Kenneth looks up to the bright shining stars.

God give me a sign. Help me with this decision. What shall I do?

Kenneth notices a small falling star in the distance, then another, followed by two more. He witnesses a ten-second meteor shower.

The heavens are crying for a people who cannot free themselves from the iron fist of a foreign ruler.

A smile appears on his face.

Kenneth returns to the celebration and immediately approaches Colonel Wood, Lieutenant Colonel Roosevelt, Captain Salvatory, and Father Ortega.

They are all standing in the center of the compound near a large bonfire that is lighting up the night sky when Kenneth says, "Colonel Roosevelt, I have given this offer from the president much thought, and I believe that I would like to join your expedition if the offer still stands."

Teddy extends his hand to Douglas and, with a huge smile, says, "Hell yes, son."

Chapter 25

The desert is cool and quiet as Mother Nature allows just a touch of that coolness and quietness to sneak into our camp—well, at least until Nagel starts blowing that horn of his. I awaken to his attempt at reveille, a job that no one else wanted. He made the mistake of raising his hand when Sarge asked if anyone liked music.

This is our first official day of training with our new rifles. At least we thought it would be. Just like I said when we were unloading the wagons, there are not enough rifles for everyone. Each tent received one rifle. Sarge was right: some of us would have to use our old firearms. I became the fortunate one when it was time to hand out the new guns.

Sarge put it this way. The bugler does not need a rifle. He has his hands full and should use a pistol. Scudder is used to large explosions, so he and Bade are assigned a dynamite gun, and that leaves me to get the new Krag-Jørgenson rifle. I think that I am the better shot anyways.

Some tents were assigned the new Colt machine gun. That is because they couldn't hit the barn with any kind of firearm, or a rock as far as that goes. Most of us who were issued rifles were ushered to the firing range. We are destroying our targets when Sarge calls for a break. Behind the paddocks we can hear some yelling and screaming. Slowly, one by one, we start walking over there.

Ranger Douglas has set up some kind of obstacle course. Three barrels are set in a triangle about fifty feet apart. Atop each barrel is a twenty-four-by-twenty-four-inch target attached to a hay bale. We watch as Douglas starts his horse in the bottom center of the triangle. He rounds the first barrel counterclockwise, and just prior to completing the turn, he draws his pistol from its holster and fires on the target, striking it dead center. Without slowing, he starts toward the next barrel, firing his pistol at the target that he is now approaching— another bull's-eye. He repeats this feat over and over. He puts on quite the show of riding that white horse at full gallop and shooting dead center on each target.

Teddy did not fare as well. I think I saw him fall off his horse several times before we had to return to our training.

We continue training, with each day getting more intense than the prior day. Eight-hour days turn into twelve-hour days—riding, shooting, and then comes hand-to-hand combat. We beat on each other till we cannot walk or sleep either. Every time that I roll over in my cot, I feet every muscle in my body ache as if it were one large bruise. One day, Douglas was showing us how to fend off an enemy with a knife. Heck, the four of us charged him, and all I remember is the three of us flying in all directions, except for Scudder. He kind of scooted across the dirt. Ha! A new nickname for him. Douglas looks me straight into my eyes as he reaches down to help me back up, and I think to myself, *Man, I think I have a friend for life.*

I ask what he hit me with, and Sarge says laughing, "He hit you with the bottom of his boot."

I look around at the other guys and say, "I didn't even see him take it off."

Teddy is still having trouble with that obstacle course.

Kenneth walks a painted Spanish mustang up to Lieutenant Colonel Roosevelt and says, "Teddy, this is Little Texas. He was my wife's horse, and I hope you take no offense to that; however, he is a good mustang and I think that he will be better than that quarter horse you are riding."

Douglas stands there and watches as Teddy rounds each barrel and shoots on target.

Teddy pulls up next to Douglas and says, "I cannot tell you much I appreciate this gift. I shall take great pride in taking him into battle."

Douglas smiles and walks away. This is the last time any of us saw him. It was as if he disappeared. One week here and now he is gone; however, I notice that Stalking Wolf stays. I am confused over this, but we were told to concentrate on our training.

More wagons came in from Fort Sam Houston. I think Teddy called in some favors from the quartermaster. We receive brown canvas stable fatigues and blue shirts for field service instead of the usual blue wool uniforms, but what surprises most of us was the issuance of machetes instead of sabers. You would think that a cavalry unit would be issued sabers.

We are now chasing the end of May, and we hear the rumors that Tampa is on the horizon. Imagine that—my parents and siblings are there. Tampa is the embarkation location for all troops heading to Cuba.

The twenty-sixth arrives, and we get the news: "Pack up, we are heading to Tampa in a few days. Write a letter to your loved ones if you have any, you may not have another chance. Tonight we celebrate at the Menger Hotel."

We were a bunch of enthusiastic cavalrymen as nearly fifty of us make our way to the Menger Hotel. The beer was actually cool. Some of the guys play cards while others enjoyed the company of the ladies. It was not long before Bade and Sarge head to the cantina—Mexican ladies! We all have a great time knowing, that it could be the last celebration for some of us.

Dear Mother and Father,

We have received word that soon we will be leaving San Antonio and heading to Tampa. I was told that our rail ride should last about four days. We are well prepared for our fight; Colonel Roosevelt has seen to that. I have made several friends here, and we cling to one another, knowing of the battles that await us. I believe that we are a well-trained cavalry unit. Sergeant Martin keeps us in line and focused on our mission. I have told all of the guys that maybe we can have a family barbeque before we ship out. I am so excited about seeing the two of you along with sis and little brother. The guys keep asking about sis, but I told them she is only sixteen and to stay away for her. They all laugh at me. See you soon.

Your loving son,

Charlie

The twenty-ninth arrives, and we load up on the Southern Pacific railroad and head to Tampa. A little over a thousand of us made the trip, with over twelve hundred horses and mules. We make stops in Lake Charles, Louisiana; Birmingham, Alabama; and in Pensacola before making it to Tampa via Lakeland. It was four days on the rails that I will never forget. Folks along the way come out to greet us, and they bring flowers and fruit for us. We can tell that we were approaching a town because the rails are lined with young people waving to us and holding the Stars and Stripes in their hands. It is like we were heroes, and we haven't even seen battle. I will always remember this one older lady that I saw standing along the tracks as we were passing through Baton Rouge, Louisiana. She looked straight at me and hung her head as she performed the Holy Trinity.

Chapter 26

We arrived in Tampa on June 3 and brought excitement and enthusiasm with us that spread to the other soldiers and citizens as well. The press loved us, or rather they loved Teddy. He was always down at headquarters talking about "The Rocking Chair War" as described by most of the newspapers.

When you added our regiment to the others from around the country, we were some twenty thousand strong, easily outnumbering the fifteen thousand residents of this sleepy, sandy town that lay between New Orleans and Havana. Tampa served as the third leg in a triangle of ports that exchanged products ranging from cattle to tobacco. There was no greeting committee there for us, so the officers had to search for us a place to camp and food for the night. The train just dropped us off at a place called Tampa Heights. We had no idea where we were or what we were supposed to do. It was a complete state of confusion, so we set up our tents in a sandlot just west of the military headquarters, which were in the Tampa Hotel.

We started marching the very next day. Teddy wanted to rest the horses, so they were only ridden every other day. Marching like infantry was hard on all of us, especially since we were not used to walking in our boots for any long period of time or distance.

Nights were another question altogether.

We visited a place called Ybor City just east of Tampa. It was named after Victor Martinez Ybor, who set up a cigar manufacturing center back in 1886. There were Spaniards, Cubans, and Sicilians, which made a large mix of the Latin culture there. Everywhere were signs "Cuba Libre" or "Free Cuba." Some of the guys got a little wild and shot up the saloons and raided the bordellos. Heck, they are just young guys letting off steam. We were ready to fight even if it meant each other.

To the east of our camp were four thousand black soldiers, the Twenty-Fourth and the Twenty-Fifth Colored Infantry, Second Battalion. They kind of kept to themselves for some reason. I was impressed with the way that they marched and how professional their camp was.

Tampa was really hot and humid, so in the middle of the afternoon, instead of marching, we would fill ammunition belts with cartridges just to get out of the sun and heat. A few of the days, we actually had combat training with our horses. We laid them down on their sides and shot our rifles over them at a fixed target. Only a few of the horses were shaken by the gunfire; the rest did great. I saw Miss Clara Barton and her Red Cross Volunteers walk through our camp. It seemed as if everyone was coming to Tampa for a piece of the action.

Steamers from Plant Steamship Company started showing up in the bay. We knew that our time for departure was nearing. All of the guys were keeping the camp barber busy. One day, George Jolly shot and killed an alligator and cooked it for us. He grew up in Louisiana, so I guess he was used to that kind of hunting. He died two days later after he drank some carbolic acid thinking it was whiskey.

Sunday morning rolled around, and some of the guys were feeling the leftovers of Ybor City—a night out on the town visiting the gambling shops and later seeking the companionship of a friendly face and a soft touch to take their mind off of the coming week. Word spread quickly that we were shipping out this week. The mood grew more serious with each passing day. A quiet atmosphere took over the entire camp.

Sarge and Scooter joined me for an early morning cup of coffee. We didn't talk that much. The days are approaching when we shall depend upon each other for our survival to get us through this "splendid little war" as the writer for the *New York Post* called this venture. Mid-morning found us as Nagle and Bade escaped their tent and join us as we walk over for Sunday morning service at a makeshift church that had been set up for us. The church hosted every religious belief, including Christianity, Judaism, Buddhism, Islam, and some others that had to be explained to me.

The Buffalo Soldiers (which is what everyone called the black regiments) that were camped by Robles Pond were invited by Teddy to join us this final Sunday, and most of them did. I watched a proud people march into our little church. Their heads were held high, and their shoulders were square—a very impressive group of gladiators. We took our seats on the hay bales that were brought in from the local farms. Father Hill, or as he says it, "Father James Hill, I marry them and bury them," prepared us for our finial organized religious ceremony.

I do not recall how many of us were in attendance that day, but I remember Father Hill standing up at the pulpit and saying, "As you prepare to march off into history, remember this day when men of all colors, men of all races, men of all beliefs, stood together as one with one common goal, one common quest, to free a people from the hand of a dictator so that they also may live and prosper under the eyes of our Lord."

The five of us left the services and headed south to Tampa Bay. My parents have organized a barbeque for us, courtesy of the Cary Dairy. The walk was not that treacherous through the miniature piney forest for about three miles and then out onto one of the most beautiful sites that I have ever seen. I stepped out onto the white sand covered beach and my eyes immediately fixed upon the deep-blue water as wave after wave splashed upon the shoreline. Palm trees lined the beach in each direction. In the distance to the east were two small islands standing guard over the mouth of the Hillsborough River, and to the west was shoreline lined with palm trees that stood watch over the seagulls and pelicans as they played in the crystal clear water.

My mother was the first to see us. We ran to each other and hugged till our breaths had escaped each of us. I gave my father a hardy handshake, but he pulled me into him with an embrace that I shall always treasure.

I introduced my parents to my friends, starting with Sarge. He is such a professional and gentleman. My sister and brother were also there for a family reunion that caused my mom to tear up and smile at each of us.

My sister invited her school teacher to the event.

"Charlie, this is my teacher Patricia."

I was so starstruck that I had trouble speaking. An angel was standing before me with her blonde hair hanging down to her shoulders, her sparkling blue eyes that caught everyone's attention, and a flawless face that made your breath run from you. I could feel my heart pounding and trying to escape my chest. The guys laughed at me, but I spent the entire afternoon with her walking up and down the beach, talking about nothing, just talking. I tried to hold her hand once, but that didn't work.

As the evening settled in and the sun set over the Bay, the time came for us to leave.

I asked Pat, "Maybe I can write you?"

She looked at me and said with a soft voice, "You had better write to me, if you know what is good for you."

We helped Dad load the wagon, but soon my father pulled me off to the side and away from everyone else.

"Son," he said, "be careful, this is not a Rocking Chair War as the newspapers are calling it. Men die in war. Some of your friends that were here today will not come back; just make sure that you do."

We shook hands. I think that he looked at me as a grown man that day.

Morning came early, and we headed to the rail station, where we had been instructed to go, but no trains came. Several hours passed as a northbound coal train approached us. Colonel Wood ran out and stopped the train. We loaded up and started the nine-mile trek back south to Port Tampa.

The port was an unorganized mess just like the first day when we arrived in Tampa. No one could tell us what ship to board or where to go or who to talk to. We did a lot of standing around while Colonel Wood and Lieutenant Colonel Roosevelt searched for the depot quartermaster, Colonel Humphrey. We were allotted a transport, the *Yucatan*. We were also told that 560 men and all of the horses, except for the ones assigned to the officers, would have to be left behind. I saw grown men crying when they were told that they must stay behind with the horses and mules. We were the lucky ones who got to go, or so we thought at that time.

We sailed to the cheers of a crowed harbor. Folks from everywhere came to see us off to battle. They were singing and waving flags, cheering us on. We sailed to the middle of Tampa Bay and stopped. We sat there in the bay for what seemed like days. We were cramped together on that ship with no room to move. I don't know what was worse—the smell of all those men in that sweltering heat, the smell of Scooter's Cuban cigars, or the smell of Scooter's self-expression that he has grown so proud of.

Six days passed before the order finally came down to us. Some naval officer had mistaken some of our escort battleships for Spanish warships. We were sailing off to Cuba.

Chapter 27

As we sailed southeast of Tampa, I watched as the night lights of the city slowly disappeared. I could not stop thinking of my family and of Patricia. We were cramped together like a can of sardines, the discomfort putting everyone's nerves on edge. We had little water, and the food was bad at best. The canned meat smelled horrible and tasted even worse.

Scooter commented, "I guess the horses made the trip after all."

Nagel headed straight to the side of the ship and emptied what seemed like three days of supplies that have been stored in his stomach. He is the sensitive one.

Different officers kept coming around and presenting various situations to us—problems that were outlined in the so-called book of tactics; however, it was Manuel that got our attention. He was a Cuban who was there to help with our landing in Cuba. He told us how over the prior eight to ten years that Spain had slowly stopped supporting the sugar industry and how many of the sugar plantations had been sold to American interest. That was the only way to keep them open. America has become the leading importer of Cuban goods, taking in over 90 percent of all exports and also supplying over 38 percent of imports to Cuba.

These conditions started the move for independence. A man named Jose Marti established the grass-roots campaign to seek Cuban freedom from Spain. The small war was going well until a Spaniard named General Valeriano Weyler arrived. He set up military garrisons in the rural areas of the country and herded the people into those garrisons in an attempt to starve the rebels. That move only strengthened the rebel movement. Many of the country folk died in those garrisons. Most of the Cuban elite escaped to America.

Scooter stood up. "Now I'm pissed."

His words echoed throughout our little area of the *Yucatan*. There were about twenty of us cramped together on the main deck next to the supplies that were tied down. There was really just room for about ten, but we stuck it out, not wanting to leave anyone else behind.

Manuel continued with our history lesson and why we are here to help him and his country. One thing that Jose Marti insisted upon was that the United States would not annex Cuba. He was afraid that one iron fist would replace another. That was addressed in the Teller Amendment that was passed by The US Congress prior to the start of the war that promised Cuban independence. Jose Marti was killed on May 19 three years ago at the battle of Dos Rios, Oriente Province. The Spaniards created a martyr that strengthened the cause for independence with each passing day.

General Calixto Garcia escaped his Spanish imprisonment nearly two years ago and returned to Cuba to continue the Marti cause. He fights the Spanish with few weapons and a small army; however, his will for freedom is strong. General Garcia leads the Cuban forces and also the forces of the Mambisas led by General Antonio Maceo. They are the guerrilla fighters.

"Mambisas—I do not understand that term. It isn't Spanish?" I said to Manuel, interrupting his story.

I now had his attention focused on me, making me feel a little uncomfortable.

"Señor," he said very softly, "Mambisas are the fighters from the Dominican Republic. They have come here to Cuba to help us rid ourselves of the Spanish, who control our very lives. They are named after a great Dominican hero, Juan Ethnnius Mamby. He was a Spanish officer, who defected from their army and fought the Spanish in Santo Domingo, helping Dominica realize its freedom. Many of them have joined forces with our Cuban revolutionaries for the same cause. They fight from the jungles using machetes."

Manuel made his history lesson so captivating that each morning we anticipated his new story with much enthusiasm. After a quick snack of beef on what appeared to be bread and chased with stale water, we looked forward to Manuel's words, something fresh to help us make it through the hot, sweltering day.

I could tell that our voyage must be coming to an end. Seagulls were now following our flotilla of thirty-seven ships, guarded by the battleship *Indiana* and numerous other cruisers. Another battleship, the *Oregon,* was also tagging along. It had sailed from San Francisco to the west coast of Florida to join us. That voyage took over a month and a half going around South America.

On the morning of June 22, we awoke to the sound of Navy guns blaring. Sarge was yelling at us to prepare to disembark. I could see the explosions on land and knew that we were in for a beating trying to make our way through the rough landing waters and onto the Daiquri beach front. All at once the navy guns lay silent, just as quick as they had started. I guess they completed their job because the only resistance that we had was boarding those small boats and trying to make it to land. I think the landing without any docks and the rough waters was the most dangerous part of our day. We all took three days of rations—well that is what we were told they were—and as many ammunition belts as we could carry and walked the last hundred yards onto shore.

The landing took all day. I'm just glad the General Garcia and his forces were there in Daiquri covering us so that we could set up our camp safely. The regulars under General Shafter were landing at Siboney, seven or so miles closer to Santiago. I bet they were not eating canned beef.

The landing could have been comical had it not been so tragic. The supply guys had it the hardest. We made it ashore a hundred yards, and I saw Marshall, Teddy's assistant, hanging onto the mane of Little Texas as they came ashore. We lost most of the pack mules. They were loaded down with supplies and just could not make the swim. The packs were cut from their backs and brought ashore. We sat on the ground of our temporary camp and watched the locals taking the bodies of those animals away.

Scooter was always the one with a wise crack. "More canned beef tonight."

Night fell, and we had our little campfire going. I remember Sarge telling us about some disease called yellow fever. He did not know exactly what it is but said that in the tropical areas like Cuba that we need to be aware of our surroundings and avoid the mosquitoes. Symptoms were fever, headache, chills, back pain, loss of appetite, nausea, and vomiting.

Bade yelled to Sarge, "We all have yellow fever after that trip we just made."

Not a good move on his part! Nevertheless, I made sure that I was downwind so that the smoke could keep unwanted guests from my tent. I took advantage of the time and wrote a letter.

My Friend Patricia,

We have landed in Cuba and have made it safely ashore after fighting our way through some rough and turbulent waters. We have not encountered any enemy resistance from the Spanish; however, with no docking facilities here, we had quite the adventure coming ashore. One of Colonel Roosevelt's horses did not fare well and was lost trying to swim ashore along with several of the pack mules.

Cuba is, at least from what I have seen to this point, very beautiful. Our landing beach reminds me so much of our time in Tampa and our walk along Tampa Bay. I would like the opportunity to call upon you again when this war comes to a close.

Your friend,

Charles Santana

First United States Volunteer Cavalry Regiment

Chapter 28

A few days passed, and we were ordered to march down this little wagon trail toward some town called Las Guasimas. Four volunteers were needed to walk point ahead of the columns; back in the American Civil War days they called these guys skirmishers. Bade raised his hand.

"I volunteer; I will go." And off he went.

He looked back at us and said, "I'm going to be famous."

I did not feel comfortable about our little expedition being separated from the main force; however, we were there to do a job. Manuel was assigned to General Wheeler and another man named Jose was assigned to us.

We started our journey and soon had to divert through the jungle in order to get to a camping area before our attack. It appeared that the Spanish forces left our landing area and were heading to some small town just a few miles inland, and it was our job to engage them so that the main force can make haste to Santiago. It was not to long till we started noticing posters and pamphlets attached to some of the trees. The guys were grabbing every one that we came upon and asking me what it said.

Se Busca Vivo o Muerto por Crimenes Contra el Gobierno Espanol. El Diablo Blanco.

I read it aloud so that everyone could hear me. "Wanted dead or alive for crimes against the Spanish government. The White Devil."

I turned immediately and looked at Jose, but he just stared back at me without saying a word. We once again continued our journey through the jungle. It was so dense that we could have lost several men or they could have just run off—we would never have known it. We reached an open area, and Sarge told us to stop here for the night.

We all settled in around our makeshift campfire. I made it a point once again to sit downwind so that the smoke from our fire would fight off the mosquitoes and any other menacing creatures that happened to wander into our hotel under the stars. The only problem was that Scooter sat upwind from us, intentionally exposing our nostrils to those deadly fumes that he is so proud of. Nagel sat next to him, and they laughed at me while blowing their cigar smoke toward Sarge and me.

I studied Jose as he sat next to the fire with a cigarette hanging out of the left side of his mouth; he stirred the campfire with a stick as the ashes danced into the night air in an attempt to distract our minds from our current mission. He was a man of about forty years of age—a hardened man from the many years of fighting in Cuba and a Mambi from the Dominican Republic there to help free a nation. The battle lines that ran across his face showed his experience; his callused hands showed his determination for victory. I, we all, listened intently to his broken English as he started his story of El Diablo Blanco. He cleared his throat just one time and silence fell on us. Then, with a deep voice that echoed throughout the encampment, he spoke.

"My friends, this is no ordinary man but a man who inspires all of us. He is a white man much like you but different in so many ways. He has hair the color of our white beaches, and his eyes are the color of our ocean, but his heart has been taken from him; his soul is driven by some unknown force that guides him through his battles with the Spaniards.

"Just a few months ago, he came to Cuba by escaping your blockade. It was as if Colonel Quijano was expecting him. He immediately began to teach us, to show us how to fight the Spanish with little or no weapons at all. It was at the battle of Chambas that the Spanish gave him that name, The White Devil."

I interrupted him, "How can you fight the Spanish with little or no weapons?"

He stopped playing with the campfire and looked directly at me.

"My friend, El Diablo taught us to use our hands and our feet as clubs, as weapons; but most of all he taught us to outthink the Spanish. I remember the first night that he was with us. Five of us surrounded him and charged him to show the Colonel that we do not need his help, that we are strong fighting Mambises. I was lying on my back when he extended a hand down to me to help me up. I sat there and looked around as my partners were also attempting to regain their senses. That is when my niece, Lisa Rodriquez, walked right up to him and slapped him across the face, and said, 'you are here to help us, not hurt us.'

"Lisa is a twenty-two-year-old from Santo Domingo, Dominican Republic. She came to Cuba with her older brother Juan to help in Cuba's fight for independence. Juan was killed along with Antonio Maceo in the machete charge, a noted Mambi battle. She is five foot, three inches tall and weighs next to nothing. Her long black hair extends down past her shoulders and halfway down her back. Her mocha-colored skin is flawless and causes her smile and big brown eyes to stand out, drawing everyone's attention when she is in your presence.

"I watched him as he looked at her with an astonished expression, and she stared back up to him. It was as if their movements were frozen. They formed a unique bond, a relationship that keeps the two of them together every day and every night.

"I don't even know what his real name is. I just heard Lisa calling him Amante. I am sorry, my friends, I have digressed," he said, looking around at us.

Jose had all of us eating out of his hands, waiting on his next word. He continued as other Rough Riders joined us. Two dozen had now gathered around our little outdoor theater.

"Colonel Quijano told us that we had only a short time to learn the Generalissimo techniques that Amante, El Diablo, was here to teach us. No time was being wasted; we started that very moment with hand-to-hand combat, then proper use of the machete as an offensive weapon. The majority of us had only used a machete to cut sugar cane or tobacco leaves.

"I have never seen a man, a human man, fight with such effectiveness. El Diablo's hands are fast and accurate. He taught us how to block attacks from soldier's rifles with bayonets attached to them, how to use our weight as counter measures, and how to kill just using our hands. The machete is heavy for us, but he twirled it like a twig, a small stick, and then he pointed out the deadly targets on a man's body to strike. Like I said before, he is not like any of us, any of you.

"El Diablo taught us to learn the movements of the Spanish supply wagons. He said to stop fighting like an equal army and to work in the cities to learn whatever intelligence we can. He and Lisa disguised themselves as husband and wife both working at Señor Carlos de Cespedes plantation, our secret headquarters. I believe that is the only time I have ever seen him smile was when he was with her.

"We soon moved all of our family members into safe areas. Any family member who fought for the revolution meant danger to the remaining family members from the Spanish General Valeriano Weyler.

"General Weyler established the *Reconcentracion*, which forced the people living in the rural areas of Cuba to be gathered up by whatever means necessary and moved to the cities. Large concentration facilities were established, and people were forced to live in conditions that caused sickness and death. Many died from mass starvation; however, the Spanish continued this plan in an effort to reduce the support for the revolution. It only served to ignite our cause.

"Each day, we planned an attack on a supply wagon at some location that would be beneficial to us. We needed weapons and supplies, and the only way that we could get them was to attack the wagon supply trains. Soon, it became apparent to me that the relationship between El Diablo and Lisa is more than that of a disguise.

"Lisa came to me one day and said, 'Papi, I need to talk to you about Amante.' She called me Papi because I am the only family that she has still alive, just as she is my only family."

We moved closer to hear his words and to hear him tell his story. Nearly fifty Rough Riders had now gathered around our theater. The only sound is occasional flatulence from Scooter.

"She said, 'Papi, I think that I have fallen in love with Amante.' She looked up to me with those big brown eyes and spoke in that girlish voice.

"I told her that he is a good man, a troubled man, a man that will take care of you, my niece.

"She smiled and said, 'Thank you, Papi. I love you.'

"Women in the Mambi fight alongside the men, and Lisa is no different. She trained with us and went on missions with El Diablo just like the rest of us. I remember in one of training sessions he was teaching us to disarm our opponents and then kick them in their midsection; he turned around, and she kicked him below his belt. She is so much shorter than he is. He fell to the ground, and she ran over to him to make sure that she did not hurt him. We all laughed.

"We work the plantation, cutting sugar cane while El Diablo and Lisa drive the wagons into Chambas to the factory. It is their responsibility to meet with the Catholic priest and gather any intelligence they can. El Diablo has to wear a long black hooded cloak over his clothes to hide the color of his skin anytime he is out during the day. If the Spanish soldiers recognize any gringos, they immediately put them in prison camp.

"It was one month before you Rough Riders arrived when he and Lisa drove the wagon back to the plantation and informed Colonel Quijano that General Weyler and his troops were heading to Chambas. We had to make plans to move. There was just no possible way that we could survive fighting against his army. We needed to move into the jungle, farther away from the city."

I looked around our little "hotel" and nearly a hundred Rough Riders sat there listening to Jose, and others were walking our way. He took a big draw on his cigarette then continued.

"General Weyler was closer than we thought. We did not have time to leave before his troops attacked the plantation. They must have known where we were and came straight to the plantation. I was inside one of the barns when I heard the first rifle shots, the screaming and the yelling from the women, from the children. I will never forget those sounds. We ran in all directions, and they kept shooting. El Diablo was in the south fields miles away and was not there when the attack started. Lisa came running out of the main house and was one of the first ones captured. I have not seen my niece since that day.

"I ran out the back of the barn and into a wooded area. I saw men with their hands up in surrender being questioned, then shot. This went on for what seemed like a lifetime, but it was only two hours. I watched as General Weyler split his troops. He had two squads take the prisoners into Chambas while he and his remaining troops headed east, killing any Mambi they came across.

"I am ashamed of my action or lack of action that day. I saw my niece taken away, screaming and fighting, yelling for her Amante. I watched all of them leave before I finally walked out of my tree-covered hiding place."

I watched as Jose hung his head and took another draw from his cigarette. A tear escaped his eye and ran down his face. He took a deep breath and continued.

"Three hours had passed and I was checking the dead, but there were no survivors. Their bodies just left there for the night scavengers. El Diablo arrived with six others. I watched his face as I tried to explain what had just happened, what I had witnessed. I could tell that his mind was racing, his blood boiling, his hands clinched in fists. I told him they took Lisa to Chambas.

"Night was now chasing the day away, and I tried to stop him, but he left. He would not allow any of us to go with him; he just said, 'Go to Remedios and meet with General Gomez.' The remaining Mambi followed his instruction and headed out to join General Gomez. I stayed behind because I knew he was going to get Lisa."

Jose had all of us on pins and needles by this time. I watched as he finished his cigarette and then flicked it into the campfire. Scooter handed him a cigar, and we sat there intensely waiting for him to continue.

"I followed El Diablo into the city. 'She is my niece, and I am going with you,' I told him. He looked at me and did not say anything.

"We arrived in Chambas. The only light was coming from the temporary holding cells set up to house the fifty or so prisoners taken from the plantation. Colonel Quijano and approximately twenty Mambises arrived as we stepped into the street. They rode their horses straight to the garrison. The warning bugle sounded, and gunfire erupted from everywhere. It was like a fireworks display. Soon, we were all fighting in the streets. They had us outnumbered one hundred against twenty-two of us. They had rifles with bayonets; we had machetes. They were pushing us toward defeat.

"I remember seeing El Diablo with a machete in each hand, swinging them like sticks. One Spanish solider would fall, then another. I said to myself, *He is like—like a Santeria Devil.* Blood was flying in all directions. We stopped fighting and just stood there as he took on the entire garrison. He went inside the building chasing some of the Spanish. I could hear the yelling, the screaming, just like at the plantation earlier in the day.

"All of the sudden, a solider is flying out of the doorway and lands at our feet on his back.

"'¿Donde esta Lisa?'

"El Diablo is standing in the doorway with both machetes raised above his head, yelling to this young soldier of about sixteen years of age like some madman, like he is possessed by the devil. The soldier is crying and saying that he does not know a Lisa or where she is. Colonel Quijano shouts to El Diablo to stop."

Jose took a long draw on his cigar. My hands were sweating, and my heart was pounding. I felt as if I was right there in the battle, watching and listening to every moment.

Jose looked around the camp and said, "My friends, this man, this American man's hair that was white is now blood red; his face and his clothes are stained with the blood of many Spanish soldiers."

He continued.

"The young soldier looked up to Colonel Quijano and said, 'Please, Señor, do not let this El Diablo Blanco kill me.'

"The colonel looked down upon the scared young man and said, 'Get up and go to your general. Tell him of this night. Go now; before I change my mind and have El Diablo Blanco send you to hell with the rest of your friends.'

"The young soldier ran off. El Diablo stood there silently. He dropped both machetes and hung his head. I do not know how many soldiers he killed that night, maybe fifty by himself. I do know this, and that is we would have all died that night if it were not for El Diablo. He saved us all. There were no prisoners there; they had been moved before we arrived.

"During the next several days, we started seeing those wanted posters that you Rough Riders have been collecting and asking about."

You could have heard a pin drop. The only sound came from the crackling of the wood. It was time to get some rest before our first engagement with the Spanish. Jose promised to continue his story the next night.

The morning came early, and I was awakened by the sounds of Nagle empting his insides. He must still have been feeling the beef.

Those navy guns soon started, and I could hear their shells finding their targets some two miles from us. Sarge was once again yelling at us, as the battle had started, and we had taken some of the side trails toward our battlefield.

Marching through the narrow jungle was hard on us, being a cavalry unit; the majority of us were not used to these long walks. We finally came upon a clearing, and a hail of bullets started popping all around me.

Sarge was yelling at the top of his voice, "Take cover! Take cover!"

I dropped to the ground as some of the others guys tried to hide behind a tree. The smokeless powder that the Spaniards use in their Mauser repeater rifles and the thick underbrush made it difficult for us to find them, much less shoot at them. In the open fields the grass was three to four feet high. We had been ambushed—walked right into a trap while trying to get to the regulars and the main battle.

We kept trying to attack the Spanish from the front and the right flank, but every time, we were sent back. I kept seeing Rough Riders fall to the ground, and then another one would take his rifle and keep firing. The Spaniards would fall back every time they sent us down or stopped any kind of offense we attempted. Every turn we made, it seemed as if they were there waiting on us. We inched forward toward the regulars. My mind drifted to the front guard and Bade. *Was he okay? Was he alive?*

I heard yelling and screaming to my right. Rough Riders from all around me stood up and charged the blockhouse that was atop the hill in front of us. I too jumped and ran, screaming as loud as I could. To my right I saw Colonel Wood and other Rough Riders charging the blockhouse. We followed Lieutenant Colonel Roosevelt as he led us up the small hill to the same blockhouse. Not a time did any of us stop to fire back at the Spaniards. We got to within several hundred yards of the blockhouse and all of the machine-gun firing stopped. The Spaniards were running out the back down the hill and away from us.

There were many deeds of heroism this day. Major Brodie was shot in the leg and kept firing. Several other Rough Riders fell to the ground but somehow continued their assault firing from the ground and one even while the medic was working on him.

Twenty-six-year-old Eric Bade was the first Rough Rider killed by the Spanish. He was at the front, leading our guys when the Spanish opened up on us. He was shot in the chest at the start of the ambush and fell to his knees with his back against a tree. He managed to fire his one hundred rounds of ammo back at the Spaniards while protecting his group. He saved the lives of many Rough Riders this day at the cost of his own.

We buried Eric Bade and the others right where we fought the Spaniards. Each Rough Rider was wrapped in a cavalry blanket and buried side by side in a long trench. Lieutenant Colonel Roosevelt placed a First United States Volunteer Cavalry Flag on a rifle and then stuck the bayonet into the ground. The chaplin said some nice parting words, and then he marked each grave and noted the location for the records.

We all lined up as a volley of rifle fire saluted our departed brothers. Nagel attempted to play taps for them, but his coughing and hacking keep interfering with his attempt. My father was right; this war had touched my group of friends.

Changes in our administration followed the next day. Colonel Wood was promoted to general and placed in charge of the entire second brigade—the dismounted cavalry—which included us. Lieutenant Colonel Roosevelt was promoted to colonel and placed directly in charge of the Rough Riders. Captain Salvatory was promoted to lieutenant colonel, bypassing the rank of major and is placed second in command of the Rough Riders.

We also got word that the Spanish have retreated back to some hill just outside of Santiago and that we will be getting a few days rest.

Sarge yelled at us, "Write your family! You may not get another chance!"

That really hit home with the loss of Bade.

My dear Patricia,

These last two days have been extremely rough on most of us. We marched from Daiquiri to a small village called Las Guasimas, where we were ambushed. I am all right. However, we lost Eric Bade in the battle. He is the one with the short, blond spiked hair, who always wore a big smile on his face. My father was right when he said that some of my friends would not be coming home. I just hope that Eric is the only one, but I know that others will be killed in this war.

Along our journey we found wanted posters that the Spanish placed on trees. There is a local hero that the Spanish have named El Diablo Blanco, The White Devil. It seems that he is giving them quite the time with his little band of fighters. Jose, our Dominican guide, has told us about his reputation and has promised to entertain us more with his exploits.

You are in my every thought. I cannot wait for the time to come when this war ends and I am able to find my way back to you in Tampa. Please pray for the Rough Riders as we march through Cuba and on to victory.

With thoughts of you,

Charles Santana

First United States Volunteer Cavalry Regiment

Chapter 29

Our few days of rest were welcomed by all. This was the rainy season, so every afternoon we saw huge dark rain clouds pop up over the coast and race from the east to the west throwing heavy buckets of water down upon us. It did not matter how hard we tried; everything got soaked. Keeping the ammo dry was a high priority. After the rains left, the sun baked us for hours, and the humidity was just unbearable. Every night, I sat downwind from the campfire so that the smoke will keep the mosquitoes from covering me. There are so many of them and, as Scooter says, "They are big enough to grill."

I had the opportunity to talk with Jose again about the local hero, El Diablo Blanco.

"Señor Santana, El Diablo is not local—he is an American like you."

My jaw dropped, and my mouth popped wide open after Jose told me that. What American is here fighting with the guerillas? My mind was racing, but I could not think of anyone. I did not remember him telling us that before.

"Señor, El Diablo is a local hero because not only does he fight the Spaniards but he cares about the people who he is fighting for. He has become one of us. I know he will find my niece. I have not seen him since you Rough Riders arrived, but I know he is seeking her and the others who were taken that day. He will not stop till he finds her, even if it costs his life. He is that kind of a man, a godsend for us."

I walked back to my tent and sat down with Sarge, Scooter, and Nagel. Nagel got up every morning before sunrise and went to sleep after sunset, taking no breaks during the day. His eyes were bloodshot, and he just looked exhausted. I knew that at 0600 in the morning he would be blowing that damn horn.

Colonel Roosevelt and Lieutenant Colonel Salvatory were in the command tent planning the upcoming events and what might be expected of us Rough Riders.

*   *   *   *

"Sal, you are the only regular assigned to this unit; however, General Wood and I wanted you as second in command because we wanted someone who has proven himself in the field of battle. Your promotion may only be a battlefield commission; however, if we make it through this little war, I will push to make it permanent."

"Thank you, Colonel; I will do my best for you and the boys."

Colonel Roosevelt's assistant, Marshall, walks into the command tent. "Colonel Roosevelt, may I interrupt you?"

The colonel looks up from the table that he and Lieutenant Colonel Salvatory are standing over and studying a map and says, "Yes, Marshall, what is it that I can help you with?"

Marshall takes a deep breath. "Colonel, first of all congratulations on your promotion to colonel and you also Lieutenant Colonel Salvatory. Sir, I have a dispatch for you from San Antonio."

"Thank you, Marshall. Sal, please stay here a minute."

Colonel Roosevelt opens his dispatch, a letter from the Mission of the Son. He reads the dispatch and hangs his head as he hands it to Lieutenant Colonel Salvatory.

Lieutenant Colonel Theodore Roosevelt

First United States Volunteer Cavalry Regiment

Cuba

I hope that this message finds you in good health; however, it is with great sorrow that I write to you.

June 1, 1898, is the day that we celebrated the life of Miss Rose Garcia as she has journeyed to join her daughter and granddaughter. Five days later, Father Ortega joined her on that journey.

Ranger Douglas instructed me to correspond directly with you, so if he is still alive, please relay this information to him. Both have been buried next to his family.

Stalking Wolf

Chieftain

Lipan Apache Nation

Salvatory looks over to Colonel Roosevelt and says, "Douglas just cannot get a break in his life."

Roosevelt turns slowly back to Salvatory, an expression of sorrow upon his face.

"Sal, I made a promise to him back in San Antonio, and by God I plan on keeping it. What is the latest news on his efforts? Do we have any updates?"

"I talked with General Gomez late yesterday. He advised that all of his forces have been brought here to join the American expedition with the exception of Douglas and five others. He instructed Douglas to disrupt as many of the supply lines as possible. I think he has been sent to find the fifty prisoners from Chambas. They may have been taken to Santiago, if they are even alive at all."

*   *   *   *

We were awakened by Sarge early in the morning of July 1.

"No reveille today; we're too close to the Spanish lines," he said.

Scooter and I immediately got up, but Nagel remained on his blanket. He was covered with sweat and shaking. I called for Sarge to come back.

He said, "Charlie, you and Scudder take him to the infirmary and hurry back."

We threw his arms over our shoulders and basically dragged him a couple of hundred yards to the infirmary. The medics looked at him and started the IVs in both arms.

We left him there, but we told him, "Glenn, we will check on you first chance we get."

Scudder and I ran back to our tent.

We got back just in time for a cup of coffee and a piece of stale bread before we had to roll up our bedding and get to formation.

We were soon marching toward Santiago, and my feet were killing me—cavalry acting like infantry.

Tampa Heights to San Juan Heights!

San Juan Heights overlooked Santiago and was defended by some one thousand Spaniards. Two main hills protected Santiago. On the first was an old sugar-processing plant with large kettles—processing cauldrons—atop the crest.

As Scooter said, "Ahh. Kettle Hill."

The larger hill was called San Juan Hill by Sarge, as it looked right down to Santiago. The hills did not really have names; they were just something we made up to entertain ourselves. We finally reached our destination and were told to take it easy and relax.

"Our artillery is going to wish them a good morning."

I watched the sun peek its face over the San Juan Heights just when I heard the battery of artillery fire over our heads toward the Spanish lines. That sound is hard to describe; it's a high-pitched whistle from behind you and then over and away from you as the shell flies to its target. I was just amazed at it—well, that was until that sound started heading back at us.

"Run for cover! To the left five hundred yards! Run!" Sarge was shouting and waving his arms at us.

A couple of the shells landed close, and we lost a few of the guys, but the majority of us made it away from their bombardment and out of their range. This exchange went on for a couple of hours before the Spanish guns were silenced.

We stood there, 480-plus of us Rough Riders, ready to push the Spanish to surrender in Santiago.

Is this the day?

Some fifteen thousand American troops were ready and willing. We got the word that General Lawton's infantry were involved in a heated battle over at El Caney, just ten miles from us. We started marching toward that Kettle Hill, taking cover along the bank of the San Juan River. We soon found ourselves pinned down, trying to avoid sniper fire. Captain O'Neil was walking back and forth in front of us. I saw him fall victim to a Spanish bullet.

The Spanish regulars and their guerillas were shooting at us from the jungles, behind trees, and from a blockhouse atop the crest. Every time one of us tried to look for a shot, some bullet would find its mark. Something had to happen; otherwise, we would not see the sun set this day.

*   *   *   *

"Colonel! Colonel Roosevelt! Over here—you need to see this," Lieutenant Colonel Salvatory shouted, looking toward the blockhouse through his spyglass.

Colonel Roosevelt took the spyglass and looked to the crest of the hill. Five Mambises and one other man wearing a black hooded cloak were attacking the Spanish regulars from their rear—a suicide move. They fired point blank on the Spaniards and then drew their machetes and engaged in hand-to-hand combat: one thousand Spaniards fighting against six patriots.

*   *   *   *

Colonel Roosevelt tossed the spyglass back to Salvatory and immediately yelled to the squad leaders, "Charge the hill, men! Charge the hill!"

He was atop Little Texas and was waving his hat back and forth. We jumped to our feet and charged Kettle Hill, yelling along with Teddy as loud as we could. We were running so hard and dodging bullets that we did not even attempt to return fire. I don't know what distracted the Spanish from firing on us, but all of the sudden we were not dodging as many bullets as before.

We reached the crest of the hill after cutting our way through barbwire, when I saw Colonel Roosevelt dismount Little Texas and continue on foot. A bullet had grazed his elbow; however, two had struck his horse. The Tenth Cavalry Buffalo Soldiers were fighting along with us, and thanks to them we were able to secure the right side of the hill. We all jumped into the trenches and tried to get a peek over the top at the action as the Spanish retreated up San Juan Hill.

"Señor Charlie! Señor Charlie!" Jose shouted as he ran toward me. "Señor Charlie, they have taken him—the Spaniards have captured El Diablo!"

I looked toward San Juan Hill, and I could see several Spanish regulars dragging a man by his arms into one of the blockhouses.

"Colonel!" Salvatory yelled.

"Yes! I saw them! Prepare the men for attack!" Teddy shouted back to his second in command.

The Twenty-Fourth and Twenty-Fifth Colored Infantry had secured the center portion of the hill. They were soon joined by the Tenth Cavalry and a feisty lieutenant, Black Jack Pershing. He had them on their feet and advancing at the same time Lieutenant Colonel Salvatory gave us our orders to advance. Once again we were running up hill, yelling and screaming and cutting our way through more barbwire. We stopped only to fire on the Spanish still in the trenches as we reached them. Soon, the entire American expedition was racing up San Juan Hill.

We reached the crest of the hill after cutting our way through more barbwire and jumping over trenches. The Spanish had retreated down to Fort Canosa, which stopped us from marching right into Santiago. The hills channeled down to a small valley, and at the far end of that valley was Fort Canosa. It looked like an old Spanish blockhouse with cannons sticking out over the top and rifle ports in the closed wooden windows. The fields that led up to the fort were shaved down so the Spaniards could see anyone approaching from any angle or distance. We were being fired upon by artillery from Santiago; however, we were pretty much out of their range, and once General Wood sent up reinforcements to us, we were able to secure our position. We found dead Spanish regulars alongside guerrilla fighters.

We were just getting settled in when the Spanish began a counterattack. Luck was on our side as the Gatling guns have made it to the crest along with Scudder and his dynamite gun, "Dinah." Once they opened up with a strong volley, the charging enemy quickly retreated back toward their fort of safety.

Our victory at San Juan Heights allowed us to establish a strong hold around Santiago. Our navy was waiting off shore for any attempt from the Spanish to leave by means of the sea. I could not help but think of what was happening inside that city. Several small battles occurred over the next several days, but the enemy was quickly turned back to the city.

About the seventh day, we saw a couple dozen people leave the city and walk toward us. Jose and some of the other Mambi ran toward them.

I thought we had better get ready for another attempt by the Spanish to dislodge us from our position. That was not the case, however. I watched Jose as he ran up to a little female, and she ran to meet him.

"Lisa! Lisa, my baby, you are alive!"

They hugged as the others all came together. The prisoners had been released.

Jose introduced me to his niece, "Señor Charlie, this is my niece Lisa."

I looked at her, and she smiled and thanked me and the other Rough Riders for helping her and her people. She began to tell us about her journey since her capture at Chambas.

"We walked for what seems to be the entire country. They used us for bait trying to lure Amante into a trap, but my Amante is too smart for them, and this angered the Spanish general. He has lost many men trying to capture my Amante.

"When we heard the cannon fire it, was obvious to us that you Rough Riders were near. Amante told us that you were coming."

She turned and gave Jose a big hug as tears fell from her eyes. Teddy and Salvatory stood right there, listening to every word as intently as we were.

"Please continue, Miss Lisa," Teddy asked her, "tell me about Captain Douglas. Are they holding him in Santiago? Is he alive?"

My mind started racing, *Captain Douglas—an American fighting here in Cuba—Texas Ranger Douglas.*

She released her hold on Jose and turned to Teddy, "Señor Colonel, they made us watch as they tortured him. We were brought into a large auditorium. He was tied to a chair, and the general was yelling at him, then he ordered one of his men to pour something onto Amante's right hand. I could smell his skin burning, but he did not scream; he would not give them the satisfaction of knowing that he was in pain. They kept hitting him, striking him across the face over and over. I could not watch my Amante.

"As Amante was about to pass out, the general had his men pour water onto him to try and keep him awake. They then released him from the chair. His hands and feet were bound as they raised him into the air by a rope over some makeshift hangman's torture chamber. I thought they were going to hang him, but he just hung in the air."

Sarge offered her some water, and she drank, thanking him for his kindness. Then, she continued.

"One of the men took a whip and wrapped barbwire around the lead and started striking Amante across his back, then his stomach. Blood was running down his whole body. The general would order his man to stop and then yell to another one 'de agua salada' (salt water). They were pouring salt water onto my Amante's open wounds. I cried and cried, but they continued to whip him over and over, stopping only long enough to pour more saltwater into his open wounds."

She once again fell into the arms of her uncle. She was crying and I could see Teddy getting mad as anger was taking over his emotions.

"Miss Lisa, do you know if he is alive?"

"Señor Colonel. That is the question that haunts me. They led us away and continued their torture of Amante. A few days later, they opened the doors to the Fort and sent us out here."

July 17 came, and the Spanish surrendered. We entered Santiago, and Lisa took us straight to the auditorium where Captain Douglas was being tortured. Colonel Roosevelt entered first, and I was not far behind. The smell of death lingered in the air. I looked around and saw sights that will remain with me forever.

In the center of the large room were a table and a hangman's stand. A rope was hanging down from the crossbar. On the table was the bull whip with barbwire wrapped around the lead, just as Lisa had described. There were pieces of human flesh on the barbs, and next to the whip was a bottle marked "acido sulfuric" (sulfuric acid). Several buckets of water were on the floor by the back side of the table. There were blood stains over most of the floor.

Lieutenant Colonel Salvatory looked over to Teddy and the rest of us and said, "No man could have survived this."

We walked out of the auditorium and back to the rest of the Rough Riders.

Sarge looked over to me and said, "I met him when he was eighteen years old, a young deputy just getting started."

We did not speak another word till we made it back to our camp. That was the longest two miles I ever walked in my life.

Scudder was waiting on us to return. He had been to the infirmary to visit Nagel.

"I have some bad news; Glenn passed away this morning—yellow fever."

Our hearts filled with grief with the loss of so many of our close friends.

We lost more of our men to yellow fever than we lost in our battle with the Spanish. Colonel Roosevelt got us out of Cuba with the help of the yellow press that got us into this war. As we boarded our transport, I said good-bye to my friend Jose and his niece Lisa. They were heading back to the Dominican Republic. They had lost their entire family fighting to free a nation, and Lisa lost her Amante. We left Cuba on August 7 and landed in Montauk Point, Long Island, on August 14.

*   *   *   *

After the last of the men had boarded, Lieutenant Colonel Salvatory approached the loading area.

"Colonel Roosevelt."

"Yes, Sal, what is it?"

"Sir, all of our men are accounted for except one. Captain Douglas shall be listed as missing/killed in battle since we never recovered or located his body."

*   *   *   *

My dearest Patricia,

Cuba has not been the adventure that I and so many others thought that it would be. I have lost two close friends in Eric Bade and Glenn Nagel, one on the battlefield and one to yellow fever. We are shipping out soon for Long Island before we are disbanded. I pray that no man goes through what we have during this little war.

I look forward to the time when I can step off the train in Tampa and see your beautiful face waiting there for me. I miss you so much. This war makes you give great thought to where you are in life and what you want to do with your life. I feel that we need to sit down and have a long discussion about what the future may hold for us.

With never ending love,

Charlie

Chapter 30

The morning of August 14, 1898, was welcomed with the arrival of the USS *Miami* in Long Island. I stood on deck, ready to leave my sea legs behind me for good. On land I could see our pals from Florida, the Rough Riders who were left behind, for they were waving their hats high in the air and yelling to us. I finally felt that we were safe from whatever harm this war could bring to us. I was wrong—we entered into our forced encampment.

Camp Wikoff first appeared as a godsend for us with its tens of thousands of tents, hospital facilities, restaurants, and postal services. What started out as a good idea soon turned into a nightmare for those in charge trying to keep up with the flood of soldiers returning from Cuba. The yellow press was right there with their ever watchful eye.

The first half of our thirty-day quarantine found many of the men in the hospital's receiving care for all sorts of diseases, not only yellow fever, but also "Cuban Fever" as was our name for malaria. But that was not the only sickness that we fought; dysentery was a major concern along with exhaustion. I had lost twenty pounds in weight since we had left Florida for Cuba. Some of the others had lost even more. The Rough Riders faired pretty well; however, some of the other units did not. There were men who were sent home to die.

The second half of our quarantine saw better times. We challenged other units to bronco riding. We were experienced and usually won the events without much effort. Teddy led us on a daily charge to the beach, a reenactment from San Juan Heights. The newspapers ran ads for the locals as far away as New York City to travel the one hundred miles and see "America's Heroes," the Rough Riders and Colonel Teddy Roosevelt.

The word of El Diablo Blanco had gotten out and was picked up by the *New York Sun,* which ran daily stories, mostly gossip stories about the Cuban hero. The War Department asked Colonel Roosevelt to address the media about El Diablo Blanco. I was not about to miss this circus. I, along with Sarge and Scudder, went to hear this.

Colonel Roosevelt and Lieutenant Colonel Salvatory sat at the table, ready to address the members of the media, some two dozen reporters representing local newspapers from the East Coast, the *Tampa Times* from Tampa, Florida, and several European tabloids.

"I know that you boys have heard the rumors of an El Diablo Blanco. The Cubans praise this myth, and the Spanish wanted to destroy the myth. The deeds that El Diablo Blanco committed during this little war are just too amazing for one man to have accomplished. In reality, gentlemen, El Diablo Blanco was just a propaganda campaign created by us to assist the Cuban people and their struggle for independence. El Diablo Blanco never existed."

The reporters went crazy with Colonel Roosevelt's statement that had been prepared for him by the War Department.

"Colonel Roosevelt, with all due respect, sir, we have quotes from your men. Sergeant Robert Martin states the following, and I quote him:

"'El Diablo Blanco is a name the Spaniards gave to one of our Rough Riders. He was a captain, and I use the term *was* because it appears that he has fallen victim to this war. I first met him in San Antonio, some eight or ten years ago; I am not sure. There was a gun battle in the streets, and we were both on the right side that day. He became a local celebrity after that day for his actions in that battle. You know him as Texas Ranger Kenneth Douglas.'"

The other reporters erupted with yelling and screaming. "Texas Ranger Douglas?"

Colonel Roosevelt looked to his left and whispered in the ear of his second in command, "Sal, I know that he is alive. God would not let him die. I know he is alive somewhere."

We stood there watching our leader as he looked over his audience, studying their faces, their anticipation for his next word.

"I will surely get in trouble for what I am about to say, but I have never been a man to hold back the truth. In about ten days from now, the Rough Riders shall no longer exist as we muster out of service, so what I am about to say is gospel not gossip.

"I first met Ranger Douglas in San Antonio several months ago, and like many of you I had read the articles and periodicals written on him and his adventures with the Texas Rangers. I approached President McKinley with the idea of offering Ranger Douglas a commission in the United States Army and assigning him as a special agent to the president. With that in mind, the president assigned him to me and the Rough Riders. Ranger Douglas took that assignment and was commissioned a captain in the United States Army. His orders were to go to Cuba and train the freedom fighters and assist them in disrupting the supply lines within our intended engagement areas. That assignment worked better than any of us could have imagined.

"We have documented evidence of heroic deeds that he performed during his tenure with the Rough Riders as a guerilla fighter. In the battle of Chambas, where the Spaniards gave him the nickname, The White Devil, we have eye witness accounts where he singlehandedly accounted for the death of fifty-four enemy Spanish soldiers and saved the lives of some eighty Cuban freedom fighters."

Teddy had their attention, ours included.

"General Lawton and his division attacked El Caney while we attacked the San Juan Heights. The general's unit met with heavy resistance. Captain Douglas managed to infiltrate the Spanish defenses and set off an explosion at the blockhouse that had the general's troops pinned down. That allowed General Lawton to capture El Caney and move his troops to San Juan Heights to assist our efforts."

Teddy stood from the table and walked in front of the reporters, glancing over to us as we stood to one side and listened intently. He turned back to his audience, staring straight at the reporters and continued.

"San Juan Heights—we were pinned down and being picked off one at a time. We could not see from where the snipers were shooting from with that smokeless powder they were using. Captain Douglas and his five freedom fighters attacked the Spaniards from the El Caney side of the hill. Their efforts allowed us to rally and charge the hills and push the Spanish back to Santiago. That victory set the timetable for Spain's surrender and the end of this war. Captain Douglas was captured, and his five men were killed. He was taken to Santiago, where he was tortured under the most inhumane punishment techniques ever administered under the color of war.

"Captain Douglas…" Teddy hung his head, took a deep breath, and then looked back to his audience.

"Captain Douglas has been listed as missing/killed in battle. We do not know if he is alive or dead. His body has never been found. The Spanish will not comment on whether he died when their Navy was sunk or if he was taken to Puerto Rico or if he is in a prison in Spain.

"This morning I got a message from President McKinley."

Colonel Roosevelt took a deep breath and then continued, "Captain Douglas has been awarded the Congressional Medal of Honor, posthumously."

Teddy walked out of the press conference.

One of the reporters asked me about Douglas.

I said, "Yeah, I met him. He is the kind of man who puts more into a man's handshake than some piece of medal you pin on your chest or hang around your neck."

The next morning the newspapers of the world ran the story of Douglas in the front page headlines.

A TEXAS RANGER—A ROUGH RIDER
AN AMERICAN HERO

September 15 rolled around, and I boarded a train for Tampa. My buddies Robert Martin and Cole Scudder joined me. The Rough Riders were disbanded and sent home. After four months of service in the United States Army, the Rough Riders rode off into history.

Colonel Roosevelt talked with us our last day and said to go back into American society and find a job or start a business. The war had ended, and it was time for us to get America and our families on the road to recovery and prosperity.

I started school—my father said "use your brain not your body."

Robert Martin and Cole Scudder started their own businesses: Martin, the Tampa Harness and Wagon Company on Franklin Street, and Scudder, the *Tampa Morning Tribune*, an ideal company for him and his quick wit.

Teddy ran for governor of New York later in the year and asked some of us to help with public appearances. The three of us were more than happy for a free trip to New York and the attention it brought. We were still America's Heroes and loved the attention. January 1, 1899, we stood there as Teddy is sworn in as the thirty-third governor of New York. We were so proud that a Rough Rider continued to serve our great country.

Teddy brought new ideas to an elected office with efforts to get rid of corruption and the so-called machine politics that ran the state. His ideas and efforts brought him national attention and an invitation to join William McKinley on the ticket for the Republican Party for the presidential election of 1900. Once again, we were on the campaign trail, and a successful one it was. The McKinley/Roosevelt ticket won the presidential election.

On September 6, 1901, President William McKinley was shot and died eight days later. The "Cowboy" Rough Rider was sworn in as the twenty-sixth president of the United States at 3:30 PM, the afternoon of September 14, 1901. He will "speak softly and carry a big stick."

PART THREE
PANAMA

Chapter 31

"Marshall! Marshall! Come in here, please!" the president shouts to his long-time assistant from a perch overlooking the south lawn of the White House, a scene of tranquility following a week of chaos: one president shot and killed, another entering his tenure as the most powerful person in America.

A "cowboy" (as one of the previous president's advisors calls him) steps into the stirrups, then onto the saddle as he prepares to lead a young country into the uncharted territory of world politics. Shall he ride into the setting sun after a short walk through the pasture, or shall he nurture this country so that it grows and expands, seeking its full potential?

"Yes, Mr. President?" Marshall says as he walks out onto the terrace.

"Marshall, you and I have been through many adventures together from the Wild West to Cuba. This adventure that we are about to undertake will be just as exciting if not more important."

"Yes, sir, Mr. President; what adventure are we about to undertake if you don't mind me asking?"

"Marshall, send for Lieutenant Colonel Salvatory. I have an assignment for him if he is willing to help me."

"Yes, sir, Mr. President; right away, sir."

Several hours pass as the newly appointed president sits in the Oval Office and studies papers that relate to the actions that Congress has been debating for several weeks. He has vowed to continue the practices of his predecessor; however, one item catches his eye. The route for the proposed Isthmus Canal, a path to link the Atlantic Ocean and the Pacific Ocean, is being heavily debated in Congress. One side believes that Nicaragua is the best choice, while another group pushes for Panama. Roosevelt has put great thought into this project since Congress started its debate. He sat in the Senate chambers, so he is very familiar with the political connections involved and the games being played.

A knock at the door interrupts his thoughts as Marshall enters the office.

"Mr. President, Lieutenant Colonel Salvatory is here."

"Thank you, Marshall. Please ask him to come in."

"Mr. President, Lieutenant Colonel Salvatory, reporting as ordered, sir."

The ever-professional soldier that he is, Salvatory stands just inside the Oval Office at attention and saluting the president. He receives a quick salute back from his commander and chief.

Roosevelt says, "Sal, it is good to see you, and let's dispense with the formalities."

"Yes, sir, Mr. President."

"Sal, please sit down. I have a matter that I wish to discuss with you."

Both take their seats—the president at his desk and Sal in a comfortable chair in front of him.

"Sal, this country is about to embark upon a campaign to join the world's elite as one of the most powerful nations both economically and militarily. I need your assistance. Before we entered into the Spanish-American War, President McKinley authorized a liaison, a military officer to work with the president on special assignments. You know that the only one to serve in that capacity was Captain Douglas.

"So that you know, earlier today I held a meeting in this very office. Secretary of State Hay, Secretary of War Root, Attorney General Knox, and I discussed that position. We all agreed to change your rank to full colonel and offer the position to you. Sal, there is a daunting task ahead of you should you accept, but I need someone in that position that I trust and can depend upon. Will you take the position?"

Lieutenant Colonel Salvatory ponders the offer from his friend, wondering, *What is he up to now? Whatever it is, there will be excitement and honor involved, and the betterment of our country.*

"Mr. President, it will be my honor to serve you again."

"Good. The paperwork went through two hours ago."

A smile crosses the face of Colonel Salvatory. He knows that no one can refuse Teddy Roosevelt.

The president says, "Let's get to work if you don't mind. Sal, we have a problem with that Isthmus Canal. Half of Congress wants to build it through Nicaragua, and the other half wants it to go through Panama. Heck, I don't know which one is best, but I have asked Congress, and they agreed to halt their debate on this topic until we can complete some research and get a better handle on this project. I have sent for the Walker Commission to discuss the proposed canal and their report along with their recommendation. I do know this—that someone is going to get a lot of our tax dollars no matter which way we decide, and we will be criticized for that decision long after we are gone, so let's pick the best route for America."

That night, Sal reads the report on the proposed canal and its route through Nicaragua. President Grant had authorized several studies on a possible canal through either Nicaragua or Panama thirty years earlier, and the French had even attempted to build one across Panama but stopped after just eleven miles because of disease and lack of funds. The idea of a canal across the Isthmus of Panama actually went back to 1503, when Charles I of Spain hoped to create a shortcut between the two oceans.

The United States already had an interest in Panama. A railroad was constructed from the eastern city of Colon to the Pacific coast at Panama City to ferry Americans seeking California gold. The American Indians attacked the wagon trains crossing the Great Plains, so a safe alternative was developed: the Panamanian Railroad, which was sold to the French when they started their canal expedition. The Union Pacific had already completed the transcontinental railway.

The next working day starts early—0600 hours—as the president and the newly congressionally appointed colonel sat drinking their coffee.

The president places his cup on the table, removes his glasses, looks to his friend, and says, "Sal, this is an important day for America."

One by one, the Walker Commission members arrive at the White House; however it is George Morrison who the president wants to hear from the most, for he is the only engineer on the commission and the only one supporting Panama over Nicaragua, a question that lingers in the mind of the president.

One engineer on this commission and not a one of the other members supported his research into the two proposed canal routes, the president thinks.

George Morrison begins his presentation as to why he had chosen Panama over Nicaragua. Panama is located across the equator, and thus there are not any seasonal storms like the hurricanes that our Gulf Coast experiences. This alone allows for a more stable operation of the canal. Next, there are no volcanoes located in Panama, but Nicaragua has several that could cause devastation and even termination of any efforts to build or maintain a canal. The path across Panama is shorter and thus less expensive.

Walker stands up and says, "The government of Nicaragua is friendly to the United States, and the government of Panama is controlled by Colombia. We might have to spend more money in Nicaragua, but we will only deal with one government and not two."

President Roosevelt stands and dismisses the members of the committee and thanks them for their time and efforts.

After the commission members file out, the president says, "Well, Sal, what do you think?"

"Well, Mr. President, I think that George Morrison makes the best sense from a pure engineering standpoint; however, Mr. Walker is right about the governments."

"Mr. President! Mr. President!" Marshall is shouting as he walks down the hall at a fast pace. "There has been a volcano eruption in the Caribbean; the city of Saint-Pierre, Martinique, has been destroyed."

The United States along with other nations sends relief and supply ships, but there is only one survivor.

The next week after a volcano destroyed the Caribbean city, President Roosevelt is seated at his desk opening his mail when Colonel Salvatory arrives.

"Look at this, Sal," the president says as he hands an opened envelope to his military advisor.

Colonel Salvatory takes the envelope and opens it as a small stamp falls out and onto the floor. Sal picks up the stamp, the official stamp of the Republic of Nicaragua, a landscape depicting numerous volcanoes.

"Sal, I want you to meet with Manuel Guerrero in New York City. He is from Panama. Find out just what we will need to do to build the canal through Panama. Then, I need you to travel to Panama and meet with Colombian General Esteban Huertas. He is in charge of the Colombian forces in Panama."

President Roosevelt stands from his desk and walks over to a window and looks out onto the Rose Garden. He turns slowly back to the colonel.

"Sal, if we cannot get the Colombian government to agree with us building the canal through Panama, I am willing to use that big stick for the betterment of America."

Chapter 32

Colonel Salvatory walks into the White House after being out of town for the last month and heads straight to the Oval Office.

"Mr. President, we have much to discuss."

"Yes, Colonel, we do. The Colombian government has refused to ratify a treaty allowing us to build the canal."

"Mr. President, Señor Guerrero has advised me that the Panamanian people want to separate from Colombia and are willing to assist our canal efforts for their freedom. Also, I believe for a small sum that we can buy the support of General Huertas as well."

President Roosevelt leans back in his chair and taps his hands together.

"Well, Sal, what do you recommend?"

"Mr. President, I met with General Huertas in Bocas del Toro, a small island north of Colon. He stated to me that for a small sum of American gold that he would be willing to have his troops stand down on any American-supported revolt. He would come out in support of any new free Panamanian government that allows us to build the canal. I agreed to those terms and stated that we would contact him at the right time."

"Very well, Sal. What about the interior of Panama?"

The two men walk over to and sit down at a nearby table with a map of Panama laid out atop it.

"Well, Mr. President, after General Huertas left Bocas del Toro, I was contacted by two guerilla fighters for Panama, Señor Porras and Señor Lorenzo. They advised me that they speak directly for President Navarro. I have a package here for you from President Navarro. He is officially requesting American assistance and support of a free Panama."

Roosevelt sits back in his chair and says, "That's great news, Sal. And what kind of military support do we need to provide?"

"Sir, I believe that a well-trained guerilla force inside of Panama, similar to the one we had in Cuba, is all that we will need as far as manpower."

The colonel runs his hand across the map showing the president strategic locations on the map.

"A staging of navy ships off the coast of Colon will deter any intervention from Colombia and any other South American country— 'big stick,' sir."

"You have done a fine job, Sal. What else should we do in Panama, and what do we need to concern ourselves with for the betterment of the people of Panama?"

"Mr. President, Señor Porras, Señor Lorenzo, and I discussed that very topic and a possible land invasion by Colombian forces.

"In the south, near the city of La Palma, there are native Indians from the Choocoes tribe, the Embera and Wowaan Indians. They migrated into Panama from Colombia when the Spanish first arrived in Colombia and settled in the Chepigana and Pinogana territories. The Panamanian people have been very generous to them, and they should support the Panamanian effort. The Colombians will not intrude upon them; thus, the south area should be secure except for the city of La Palma, which can be easily defended.

"Panama City is our main concern. It was originally established in 1517 and was the first city on the Pacific Coast until it was destroyed by the pirate Henry Morgan in 1671. The city was rebuilt with the White House located in the Santa Ana area. Invading forces will have to land at Balboa and Casco Antiguo in order to reach the presidential palace. Inside of Panama City are many national landmarks that President Navarro is concerned about. The Church of the Golden Altar is located near the presidential palace and holds a special meaning to his people, and we need to protect it at all costs. Below the church are dungeons and catacombs left by the conquistadors that wind and corkscrew beneath the city. We can place guerrilla fighters there to ambush any troops coming into the city.

"We also need to protect the Basilica of Santiago Apostal. It is in the town of Nata in Cocle Province and is the first church built on the American continent in 1522. In addition to the railroad, there is a secret road that runs parallel to the railway from Colon to Panama City, Camino De Cruces, which was created by the Indians. We have access to that as well. Also, the French were able to cut a path through the jungle from Colon to Panama City before abandoning their attempt at the canal, thus making movement easy for any guerrilla forces.

"Bocas del Toro is a port that is used by the Colombian shipping industry to restock their supplies. The United Fruit Company is located there, and I believe that it will support the Panamanian efforts as well. It has a small security force that tends to their needs and should help secure Bocas del Toro."

President Roosevelt once again leans back in his chair, and he says as a smile crosses his face, "Sal, I have another journey for you."

"Yes, Mr. President, what can I do for you this time?"

The president stands from his chair and grabs a package off his desk.

"Sal, I want you to travel to Fort Brooke in Tampa. There is an orphanage there run by Father Sanchez. Here is a package for someone that you will recognize. We need his help."

Chapter 33

Panama City, Summer 1902

Colombia tightens its hold on Panama, a country that won its independence from Spain eighty years prior; however, Panama is controlled by Colombia, a country that is involved in its own political battles.

"Princess Maria! Princess Maria!" the young boy shouts as he runs through the halls of the presidential palace carrying a piece of paper, which flaps in the wind. The soles of his sandals clap upon the palace pavers—they sound like two hands clapping at a flamenco dancer's presentation.

"Stop!" the palace guard commands. The young man slides on the pavers, like a train making an emergency stop upon the rails.

"What have you there?" the guard asks him. The young boy stands, looking up to the guard, his eyes wide open as he takes in all of his surroundings.

"I have a note of request of introduction for Princess Maria."

The excited young man forces the words from his body as he gasps for a breath.

The princess sits at a nearby table just inside a conference room; the double doors are opened wide, allowing the Pacific breeze to gently swirl about, attempting to chase away the heavy humidity that is upon them. She is meeting with her staff to make plans for an upcoming event that she must attend on behalf of her country. Hearing the exhausted young boy speaking to the guard, she pauses from her meeting and turns her attention to this young boy.

"Come here, young man," she says in a soft tone that places a smile onto the boy's face and a sense of comfort about him.

He peers around the palace guard, looking for the princess.

"Si, si," he says as he steps toward the princess, the palace guard walking with him.

"It is a request from Señor Kenneth Douglas to meet with the princess. He is the American come to buy our bananas, our rice, our corn, our coffee, our sugarcane, and ship it to Tampa, USA. He—"

"Stop," the princess says in a stern voice that frightens the young boy. His steps freeze upon the pavers, and the room is now silent. The princess has the attention of all her staff.

"Who is this man from America? What does he want of us? What does he want of me? I will not meet with this—this American," the princess says. "I am with my family; my sons come before any American."

The palace guard quickly escorts the young man from the secured area and away from the princess. An assistant takes the note and tosses it into a pile of papers to be destroyed.

"Captain Eduardo," the princess says in that stern Spanish voice that could awaken the most sacred of statues in the palace.

Captain Eduardo snaps to attention. He is the head of palace security, a man of vast experience in matters of national security, a man that presents himself in a highly professional manner, but also a man who knows the ways of the street and the ways of the guerilla fighter.

"Yes, my princess," he says as he stands and listens intently for his orders.

The princess stares at Captain Eduardo, her eyes like darts piercing right through him.

"This American, this Kenneth Douglas, follow him. See where he goes; see what he does; see who he talks with. This Kenneth Douglas—I no trust him."

Captain Eduardo is still at attention as the princess leaves the meeting room, followed closely by her staff. He has a look of shock over his face—the princess had never spoken to him in such a direct, forceful manner before.

Chapter 34

The Colombian ambassador sits patiently in President Navarro's chair and at his desk while the president is seated across from him in a chair reserved for visitors. The palace guards all stand at attention just outside the door, while several Colombian soldiers stand across the hallway from them.

"Señor President," the ambassador says, smirking. "The Colombian government has allowed you, and your family before you, to govern this country at our direction. We do not like the idea of the American government having any talks with you or any of your appointees without our permission."

The Colombian ambassador stands from the chair and walks away from the presidential desk, looking back over his left shoulder at President Navarro. He suddenly stops and turns back to face the president.

"Panama is part of Colombia!—or have you forgotten this?" the ambassador shouts, slamming his right fist down upon the table.

He stares down at President Navarro.

"Do we need to remind you of this? There will be no canal, period. Colombia will decide the future of Panama, not you and not the Americans."

The ambassador's face is now blood red from his shouting as both of his fists pound the table.

President Navarro slowly slides down into his chair with a defeated look upon his face.

"Yes, sir, Señor Ambassador," he says in a trembling voice, which is barely audible.

"Good, Señor President. We understand each other. Then, I shall take my leave and return to Colombia," the ambassador says with confidence.

"Yes, sir, Señor Ambassador," the president replies as he slides deeper into his chair.

The ambassador leaves the presidential office and walks down the hallway and out of the palace. President Navarro's hands clasp the end of the armrest of his chair, his fists tightening more and more till he jumps to his feet.

He quickly steps to the doorway and shouts, "Daxc! Daxc! Please come here at once!"

The presidential aide, hearing his president's voice, runs from a nearby office, "Yes, sir, Mr. President, what is it that you need?"

President Navarro looks to his aide, both hands still clasped in fists. "Daxc, I need you to contact and notify all of the cabinet members of an emergency meeting of the cabinet. I want all members here within three hours. If they ask, tell them it is a matter of great importance that they attend. I shall advise them at that time."

Daxc quickly leaves to make contact with the cabinet members.

Chapter 35

"Captain Eduardo, report" the princess, whose honorary title is given to the daughter of the president for her humanitarian work throughout Panama, demands from her spy. "What progress have you made concerning this American? Where did he go, what did he do, and with whom did he speak?"

The princess sits in her chair at the end of the room; there is a large table with her staff present. Palace guards stand at the entrance of the room, and a few servants stand nearby for assistance if needed. She leans forward, staring directly at Captain Eduardo.

"Every day for months, I have received requests from this American for a meeting," she says while holding a piece of paper in her right hand, which she waves high in the air toward Captain Eduardo. "He bothers me," she continues.

"Yes, my princess," the captain says.

He steps forward and stands at the end of the table, facing the princess. Her staff looks up at him expectantly.

"My princess, Señor Douglas took the train to La Palma. He stayed there for two days. He does not leave the hotel except at night to go to the nightclub. He just sits there at a table by himself and watches the salsa dancers. He gets up and goes to the piano and plays this American jazz. He returns to his table and talks with the people at the nightclub. The salsa dancers are all over him—hugging him, kissing him—but then he leaves with no one, not even the salsa dancers. He then takes the train back here to Panama City. My princess, Señor Douglas does not go to the fields and talk with the growers about our crops."

The captain stands at the end of the table with both of his hands now stretched out in front of him, his palms up, and a confused look spreading across his face.

"Very well, Captain," the princess says as she leans back. "Captain, watch this American. I no trust him."

She turns her head to the side and looks out a window across the hall, gazing at the beauty of her country, a country ruled over by Colombia.

The princess dismisses the captain and all her staff, and the guards return to their posts. As she looks out upon the countryside, her mind wanders.

We won our independence from Spain eighty years ago, and we have been fighting against Colombia ever since. My grandfather was killed by the Spanish. My uncle, my brother, and my husband have all been executed by the Colombian military as enemies of their state. Now my father is talking with the Americans, asking for their help. They did help Cuba.

Her mind is racing.

This American, this crop buyer, this Kenneth Douglas, maybe he can help us. Maybe he can help establish a free port of trade in Colon, and we could ship our goods to other countries, maybe we could … no! He is an American. The Americans have given Panama enough trouble with the railroad system they built here.

Chapter 36

Three hours have passed, and all of the Panamanian presidential cabinet members have assembled in the main conference room. "Señor President," the military advisor says from the end of the long table. "Señor President, the Colombian military is building strength at our southern border. I am afraid they may invade us again."

President Navarro leans forward from his chair and looks into the faces of his cabinet; his hands rest on the table just in front of him; a look of determination shines on his face.

"My friends," he says in a low, strong voice, his eyes moving from one cabinet member to another, "we have decisions to make today. The words that pass our lips this day could mean certain death to us, to our people, and to our country."

The president stands from his chair and begins to walk around the room, watching his fellow countrymen.

"For several months now, we have been in talks with the Americans to see if they can help us as they did Cuba."

The president watches each of his cabinet members for a reaction. A smile crosses the face of several members, while a look of concern darkens others.

"The Americans have offered to help us in our fight for freedom," he says, standing at the end of the table and looking directly into the faces of the concerned cabinet members.

"My friends, I know that we have had difficulties with the Americans and our railroad system that they built for us; however, we have a chance right here and now to do something for our country—to do something for our children."

The cabinet members all shake their heads in agreement with the president.

"The Americans only ask of us to allow them to build this canal, the one that the French gave up on. They want to join the Pacific Ocean and the Caribbean Sea to establish a trade route, and we, Panama, shall be the center of that route. The Americans are offering to assist us in our quest for freedom, just like they did for Cuba. I ask each of you this day to do what is right for Panama."

The president returns to his chair and sits, waiting for a reaction from his cabinet.

He watches as they talk amongst themselves. One by one, they indicate their agreement with their president.

"Good, my friends. Today we have done something good for Panama. The American warship *Nashville* and a company of American marines are sailing toward Panama as we speak."

A look of relief and joy spreads across the faces of each cabinet member.

Chapter 37

"Captain Eduardo, report!" the princess shouts as her security chief enters her private office. "Captain, this American distracts me with his daily messages. What have you learned?"

"My princess," the captain says in a low voice. He stands directly in front of the princess, and no other persons are in the room except for her confidant, Nina. "Señor Douglas takes the train to Bocas Del Toro. He stays there for two days, and at night he goes to the nightclub and watches the salsa dancers. He plays that American jazz on the piano. The salsa dancers are all over him again and again. He then talks with the people at the nightclub. He leaves by himself and goes back to his hotel room. The next day, he takes a boat to visit Balboa and Coco Solo. Once again, he does not go to visit our planters, but instead he goes to the nightclub and watches the salsa dancers and plays that American jazz. I do not like that American jazz, my princess."

"Captain," the princess says in a strong voice.

"Yes, my princess, please forgive me. I do not understand this man, my princess." The princess and her confidant look at the captain, waiting for him to continue.

"This American travels all over our country, saying he is a crop buyer from America, but he does not go to our fields, and he does not talk with our growers. Instead, he stays in his hotel room except for at night. He goes to the nightclubs and watches salsa dancers, plays that crazy American jazz, then comes back here to Panama City and stays in his hotel room."

The captain is even more confused now than when he started his report to the princess.

She thinks, *What is this American up to? What is this American doing in Panama?*

The princess and her confidant talk privately to each other.

"Page!" the princess shouts toward the opening of the room. A young man enters and runs toward her.

"Bring this Kenneth Douglas to me; we will meet tomorrow at noon. Not alone—I shall have my confidant with me."

"Yes, my princess," the page answers, and he runs quickly from the room.

Captain Eduardo stands there watching.

"My princess, tomorrow is our national holiday," the captain says with a look of concern, but the princess ignores his comment.

Chapter 38

Kenneth Douglas enters the presidential palace, flanked on each side by an armed palace guard. Princess Maria and her confidant watch as he enters her private dining room, which is located on the east side of the palace. The princess observes his every movement carefully. His footsteps barely make a sound upon the palace pavers. She sees that he is a man of strength by the way he carries himself: his shoulders are squared off, his chin up, his eyes forward. He is clearly a confident man and not some crop buyer.

Who is this man and what does he want of me? Why me?

As the princess and her confidant eye him, Nina leans over to the princess and says in a sultry voice, "Oh, my princess."

A smile comes across the face of the princess as she watches the man walking toward them.

"Nina, behave," the princess whispers to her confidant. The princess dismisses the palace guards and servants, and just the three of them remain in the room.

"Good afternoon, Princess Maria," he says in a commanding, strong voice.

He does not fail to notice her blushing cheeks, her red lipstick, and her formal white dress.

"Good afternoon, Señor Douglas. This is Nina, my personal assistant and confidant," the princess says as she gestures toward to the young woman seated to her right.

"Good afternoon, Nina," he says to her as he reaches to shake her hand.

Nina, surprised by this gesture, takes his hand, and her face flushes with embarrassment.

Chapter 39

"Señor President! Señor President!" the military advisor shouts as he runs toward the front entrance of the presidential palace, followed closely by several palace guards. They climb the steps leading into the main corridor of the building. With a look of grave concern upon his face, he shouts out again.

"The Colombian military has crossed our southern border, and they are quickly approaching Panama City. Señor President, they are killing our people, burning our homes!"

Palace guards at the main entrance open the doors that lead to the president. The military advisor yells out more warnings as he runs, but a bomb explodes, killing him and five of the palace guards. The president and a small group of men in the hallway are knocked to the floor by the force of the explosion. Dust covers them and every article in the main corridor.

The president is helped to his feet as people run to each other, trying to help the injured, covering the dead, and screaming in terror. The president wipes the dust and the debris from his clothing and turns to his American advisor, Colonel Salvatory of the United States Army. The expression upon the president's face cries for help, asks for assistance, and begs for collaboration.

"Mr. President, the USS *Nashville* has already anchored at Colon. The US Marines are headed this way, sir," Salvatory says as he too dusts debris off himself.

The president surveys the damage, the dead, and the injured in the corridor; and he listens to the voice of this American, the voice of a new friend, a voice of hope—a voice that just might be too late to save him or the princess.

Chapter 40

"Coffee, Señor Douglas?" the princess asks in a soft tone. She reaches for a decanter and then pours the steaming black liquid into the white porcelain cups on the table.

"Yes, thank you, Princess," he says in a slow Texas drawl, a voice that makes Nina look to the princess and smile.

"Please excuse me for a moment, my princess," Nina says as she stands and leaves the table. Kenneth stands as she walks away. Nina looks back over her left shoulder, smiling and winking at the princess.

Kenneth sits back down in his chair as Nina leaves the room. Just the two of them, the princess and the American, remain. The princess is not scared of this man; her two palace guards are stationed right outside the door, waiting her command.

"Señor Douglas, you are a crop buyer?" she asks very nervously.

The princess looks directly into his eyes and he into hers; neither can look away. It is as if a trance has fallen upon them, and neither knows how or why. They stare deep into each other's souls, unable to speak, unable to move, their hearts beating faster, their breaths growing short.

What spell has he cast upon me? The princess thinks. *I have not felt like this since …*

Suddenly, gunshots ring out so close that they can feel the percussion of the bullets flying through the air.

The princess stares toward the open door and drops her cup of coffee onto the table. Kenneth quickly turns, and they see two men with rifles running in the hallway, shooting at the palace guards. The guards raise their own rifles and take aim, but it is too late. The guards fall to their deaths in a hail of bullets.

The princess freezes in her chair, but Kenneth jumps to his feet, throwing his chair to one side. He reaches under his coat and produces a Colt .45, a Texas six-shooter. The strangers' eyes are fixed upon the princess, and they have turned their rifles in her direction. A gunshot rings out, and one of the men falls to his death. A second shot, and the other man is dead.

The princess, still seated at the table, looks up to the crop buyer in disbelief. He is standing in front of her and looking toward the hallway; a firearm extends from his left hand, the smoke still escaping out of the barrel.

Who is this man? What does he want of me? Why me?

Kenneth quickly turns to the princess and extends his right hand to her.

"Princess, we must go."

Still in a daze, the princess slowly reaches up and takes his hand. The look upon her face is one of shock, fear, and horror.

"I am with my family—I have two sons; they are my life," she says; her voice cracks as her eyes swell with tears.

"I know," he says in that strong, confident Texas voice. "I know. No harm shall come to you or your family." He looks down at this scared creature, whose hands shake as fear spreads across every inch of her body. "I promise you, Princess."

The princess slowly stands from the table, weak in her knees, shaken with uncertainty. Her mind races with question after question: *Who is this man, this crop buyer, this American, this stranger who has just rescued me from certain death?*

"Princess, we must go," he commands sternly.

The princess steps toward him. "My family, my sons," she says, looking deep into his eyes, into the soul of this stranger, this American.

Kenneth pulls the princess toward him, so close he can taste the mint upon her breath.

"My sons," she says again in a timid voice.

His right arm wraps around her waist, supporting her as she attempts to steady herself.

"We must go, Princess," he says again.

Kenneth holds the woman and steps toward the rear of the room, moving at a pace that forces the princess to step quickly as their hands are locked together. They move to the back hallway, the presidential hallway to the west.

How does he know of this path? she wonders. *This is private. How does he know the private path to my family, my sons?*

Kenneth hastens his pace, and the princess jogs to keep up with him.

With just a few more steps to her sons' rooms, he says, "Stop!"

Two Colombian soldiers stand outside of her sons' rooms. They have heard the princess and Kenneth running down the presidential hallway. The soldiers turn to the two of them; they raise their rifles to take aim. The couple is frozen with their backs against the stone wall of the secret hallway. Kenneth shields the princess from her assailants.

The soldiers fire at the couple, just missing them as the bullets ricochet off of the stone walls and down the hallway as Kenneth removes his gun from under his coat. He fires once, and a Colombian soldier falls dead. A second shot, and the other Colombian soldier is dead.

The princess looks to her new American friend.

Who is this man? What does he want of me? Why me?

Kenneth reaches back and takes the princess by the hand, and they run even faster than before to her sons' rooms. Stepping over the two dead soldiers, they enter the foyer that separates the two rooms. Her oldest son's room is empty. The princess immediately runs across the foyer to her youngest son's room. It, too, is empty. With no sign of either of her sons, the princess falls to her knees.

"My family, my sons, they have been taken!" she screams, her voice cracking in pain.

Kenneth searches the room of the oldest son, his eyes peering into every crack, every crevasse the way a Kansas hawk searches for a field mouse. He then goes to the room of the youngest—no bullet holes, no disarray, and no evidence of a struggle. The boys are gone, yes, but they have not been taken.

Kenneth reaches down to the princess, her head resting in her hands, tears flowing from her eyes.

"Princess, we must go."

The princess just sits on the floor, lifeless, hopeless.

"My sons have been taken by the Colombian military. They will be killed—executed—the same way my grandfather, my uncle, my family was."

Chapter 41

The sun is setting on the day of the national holiday as President Navarro and his cabinet members, the ones who managed to survive this day, are meeting in the main conference room of the presidential palace.

"Captain Eduardo, report," the president says.

He stands before his cabinet with the look of a man ready to fight to the death to save his country, his people, and his family.

"Señor President," the captain says in an excited voice, "the Colombian military has landed forces throughout our country. However, guerrilla forces in La Palma have turned the invaders back. As we speak, guerrilla forces in Bocas Del Toro, Balboa, and even in Coco Solo have engaged the enemy. All Colombian military forces are being defeated, except for here in Panama City. Colombian General Huertas has joined our fight and taken the Colombian military leaders captive. He has stopped the Colombian forces from leaving Colon."

Smiles and cheers erupt from around the table. The president turns to Colonel Salvatory, who shakes his hand, congratulating the president on their apparent victory.

The president looks back to his captain.

"Good news, my captain! Please make plans to rid Panama City of these invaders. And, Captain, what of the princess and my grandsons?" A look of great concern grows over the president's face.

Captain Eduardo steps back from the table, turns away, and looks down to the floor.

"Señor President, I do not know that answer. Your grandsons' rooms are empty, and there are two dead Colombian soldiers at the entrance to their foyer. The princess was meeting with an American, a crop buyer from Tampa."

The captain looks directly at the president, fearing he has failed his leader, his good friend.

The president's shoulders slump.

"Captain, this American with my daughter, does he have a name?"

"Yes, my president, his name is Kenneth Douglas."

The president slowly turns to Colonel Salvatory, his eyes tearing up.

"My friend, do you know this crop buyer from Tampa, this Kenneth Douglas, this man that has my daughter?"

Colonel Salvatory places his hands on the top of a chair just in front of him, looks the president straight in the eyes, and says, "Mr. President, he is the man sent by President Teddy Roosevelt to protect your daughter and grandsons. When you requested assistance a year ago, fearing that this situation might arise, President Roosevelt sent the best man for that job—an American hero, Special Agent Kenneth Douglas."

Captain Eduardo's mind races as he gathers his thoughts. *Special agent,* he says to himself. *Yes, how could I have not seen this; how could I have been so blind? The nightclubs, the salsa dancers, that crazy American jazz—the same song every time, every nightclub. He was not talking with the people at the nightclubs; he was talking with the same two men: Señor Porras and Señor Lorenzo, every time!*

"Kenneth Douglas is not a crop buyer; he was establishing the guerrilla fighters, the warriors that defeated the Colombian military," Captain Eduardo said.

"Yes, Captain Eduardo," Colonel Salvatory says. "He knew you were following him, he knew who you were, and that is why you are alive today. Special Agent Douglas sent a daily request for a meeting with the princess, knowing that she would decline. Those requests were actually messages to me, letting me know that he was successful at a particular location." Captain Eduardo falls back into a chair, astonished.

"This man, this special agent, he is good man?" the president asks.

Colonel Salvatory glances over to Captain Eduardo then back at President Navarro before replying, "Mr. President, Special Agent Douglas is the best we have. He is a private man, a soft-spoken man, a religious man, a man of God."

Colonel Salvatory's thoughts go back to a time in Tampa.

Chapter 42

One Year Earlier, Tampa, Florida

"Señor Douglas, Señor Douglas, there are men in the church office. There are military men in the church office. Señor Douglas, they ask for you. Señor Douglas, what have you done?" the young Catholic priest says as he runs across the lawn, lifting the bottom of his robe to assist his efforts, his boots pounding the earth faster and faster, looking for his friend.

Kenneth was kneeling on the ground in the construction area of the church grounds, a hammer is in his left hand and several pieces of wood are in his right. He looks at his friend, Father Sanchez of the Tampa Orphanage.

"Yes, Father," he says as he stands, dropping the hammer and the wood and then whipping the dirt and sawdust from his body. He looks to his friend and says in a soft voice of confession, "I have sinned, Father. I have killed men—many men. They are here for me."

Father Sanchez says a silent prayer for him.

Kenneth walks slowly to the church office, carrying his shirt in his left hand. Looking around the grounds, he sees young orphans playing together, not knowing what their future may be.

He glances to the makeshift church, an open-ended rival tent made from a green-canvas military-surplus field-operations command center. A wooden shed is attached to the rear, serving as an office.

Entering the church office through the west door, with the Tampa sun beaming down on his back, he quickly scans the room. Captain Salvatory, now colonel, stands to the right; two armed military guards stand to the rear; and in front stands a wet-behind-the-ears lieutenant straight out of the United States Military Academy. All of the men are trying to fend off the sun and get a glimpse at the man entering the church office.

All four men realize Kenneth is the person approaching them, and they all snap to attention—the customary salute to a Congressional Medal of Honor winner, a prize that he never accepted, never acknowledged, and never wanted for his deeds in the Spanish-American War.

"Captain Douglas," the young lieutenant says, "I have a letter and package for you from President Roosevelt."

Kenneth gives the young officer a look that causes him to shake. The lieutenant studies his hero: the bullet scar just past the right eye before the hairline; the three marks on his right hand from the Spanish acid during the torturing in Santiago, Cuba; the scarred body from the Spanish whips; the rope burn that runs from just below his belt line on his stomach to his chest. Kenneth is an American hero listed as killed/missing in battle in the taking of San Juan Hill during the Spanish-American War, but here he is standing three feet away.

"I studied you at the academy," the young lieutenant says. "Your life and service to our great country are mandatory study for all graduating officers." He goes on, excited about being in the company of his hero and actually speaking to him.

"Your exploits as a Texas Ranger, your assignment as a special agent and captain in the US Army assigned to the president, the battle at the San Juan Heights before the Rough Riders' assault, your assault on the Spaniards throughout Cuba, your capture and torture by the Spanish Military in Santiago, your—"

"Stop!" the colonel shouts.

Kenneth is halfway out of the church because he does not want or need to hear this babbling person speak of the demons that haunt him every night.

"Wait, Kenneth, please. Let me talk with you," the colonel pleads as he signals to the others to stay in the office. "Teddy needs you; we need you."

Kenneth stops in his tracks as the dust flies from the rain-starved Tampa earth below his boots; his head hangs down, his shoulders slump.

The colonel walks around to face his old friend. "There is a problem in Panama. Please take this letter and package and just look at it. Please?"

As he waits for a response, Colonel Salvatory continues, "Kenneth, you disappeared in Cuba. We didn't know if you were alive or dead.

"One report had you a prisoner in Spain, another had you killed in Santiago, and there was even one that says the Mambises had taken you back to their home in the Dominican."

Still not getting a response, he goes on. "For several years we looked for you. We have been searching everywhere for you. We heard of a man at a Tampa orphanage who had so many scars on his body that he looked as if he had been to hell to fight the devil himself. Teddy sent us here. He said, 'That has to be Kenneth. I know he is alive.'"

Kenneth slowly raises his head and looks his old friend straight in the eyes. "Teddy asks this?"

The colonel looks back to his friend. "Yes, my friend. Teddy."

Kenneth reaches for the sealed letter, taking it in his left hand and the package in his right. He turns away and starts walking back to the construction area, back to the shelters he is building for the orphans. He can hear the soldiers leaving behind him.

Kenneth sits in a small place Father Sanchez made for him. The sun has set, and the day is over. Kenneth opens the sealed letter.

My friend Kenneth,

I have enclosed in this package some information and photos of persons of interest in our endeavors in Panama. I call upon my friend simply because no other man can carry out this mission with success the way that you can. Please study these photos and the information with them, and then destroy all of the material. Colonel Salvatory shall wait for your reply at Fort Brooke in Tampa. I and the colonel are the only two people who know of this mission. Should you be captured by the Colombians, we shall deny any knowledge of this mission.

May God be with you.

Your friend,

Teddy Roosevelt

Kenneth opens the package and removes the contents: a photo of President Navarro; a photo of Captain Eduardo; a photo of Roberto, the oldest grandson of the president; a photo of Alfonso, the youngest grandson of the president; and a photo of Princess Maria, the daughter of the president.

Kenneth studies the photo of the princess. Her brown eyes, her coal-black hair to her shoulders, her flawless face; it is beauty as he has never seen before, elegance she carries so naturally. He catches his heart beating rapidly. He reads the vitae, the autobiographical sketch that has accompanied the photos of each of the subjects.

She is a single mother; her husband was executed by the Colombian military as an enemy of the state. She does not socialize except for one day a year—"The Day of the Princess," December 1, a national holiday set in her honor by the people of Panama in 1895 for her humanitarian work and education programs for children.

Captain Eduardo, head of the presidential palace security, is a career military man who is dependable, honest, and trustworthy. He has fought in many battles against the Colombian military, both as a soldier and as a guerrilla fighter. He was handpicked by the president for his current assignment.

Roberto is the oldest grandson of the president. He is fifteen years old and considered one of the best equestrian riders in Panama. He has competed successfully in South America and in Europe.

Alfonso is the youngest grandson of the president. He is twelve years old, a concert pianist, a child prodigy rarely seen in public.

MISSION STATEMENT: PROTECT PRINCESS MARIA AND HER TWO SONS AT ALL COSTS, EVEN WITH YOUR OWN LIFE.

Kenneth sits on the ground with his arms over his knees. He looks down to the earth in front of him; the only sound comes from the kerosene lantern next to him. He thinks to himself, *Even your own life. What life? I have taken so many. God, is this what you ask of me?*

Chapter 43

Kenneth reaches down to the princess and lifts her up to him. The princess glances up to her new friend.

"Princess, we must go," he says softly. "I will find your sons, Princess, but we must go." They stand next to each other as he takes her by the hand and leads her away from her sons' rooms.

They race out the back of the presidential palace and into the night air of Panama City. Sounds of war are all around them, explosions and gunfire on a day that was to be a celebration.

They run down the cobblestone street, away from the palace. Kenneth looks in every direction, listening to every sound, even the screams in the distance. He is seeking sanctuary for his princess when suddenly they come upon five Colombian soldiers slowly walking down the street toward them. The soldiers are walking in the middle of the street and looking into every storefront window they come to. They have not seen the couple.

"Quickly, Princess, in here," Kenneth says as he pushes open the double-door entrance to a storage room that is located just off the side of the street. They dive into the storage room, which is cluttered with empty banana boxes. The princess moves to the rear of the room as Kenneth closes and latches the doors. He can see out of the cracks in the wood.

The princess looks at her savior's back as he glances up and down the street. *Who is this man? Some crop buyer. He shoots a gun better than any soldier, and he knows the secret hallways of the palace. He says that he will find my sons. I believe him, this Kenneth Douglas.*

She studies every detail of him as he sits by the door: his hair is the color of the Panamanian sun, and his eyes are the color of the ocean. Every move he makes is calculated before it is engaged.

This man, this American, what kind of magic has he thrown upon me? What spell has he cast upon me? What is happening to me? He drives passion deep within me.

Kenneth slowly turns to the princess, looking over his shoulder to this beautiful creature. "They have passed; we should leave now."

She stares into his face, a battle-worn face, a face of experience, and a face to trust. A deep, warm caring for him has started to build in her heart.

"Yes, my friend," she says as he helps her to her feet.

She stumbles slightly into his arms. She feels comfortable in his arms, and their eyes once again lock upon each other. Their hearts race; their lips are just inches from each other as they begin to move closer. He cups her face, placing one hand upon each cheek. Her arms tighten around his shoulders. Their lips press gently against one another as their bodies melt together. She feels a desire, a passion, a wanting deep inside of her that she has not felt in many years.

Kenneth steps back from the princess as a smile crosses her face. He turns and opens the doors of the storage room. An uneasy feeling has taken over his body, an unknown feeling, an exciting feeling, a nervous feeling.

Stepping into the open doorway, Kenneth turns back to the princess. "We need a safe house, a safe place where I can take you that is away from all of this danger."

"My confidant, Nina," the princess says as she steps out of their hiding place and toward her friend. "Her home is by the ocean, and it is away from the center of the city."

The couple slowly steps out into the street with Kenneth leading the princess from the storage room, his hand holding hers as they navigate away from the Colombian soldiers.

Chapter 44

The backstreets of Panama City are dark and void of people. Explosions and gunfire come from the center of the city as Kenneth and the princess make haste toward the ocean.

They finally come upon a small home on the west side of the city, a modest home that overlooks the ocean.

"This is it," the princess says in an excited voice. "This is my Nina's home."

Kenneth grabs the princess by the hand and stops her as she tries to enter the house. He pulls her back to him as he surveys the house: no lights, no sound, and no movement.

Slowly and cautiously, he leads her to the rear of the house, watching for any signs of movement, any sounds. They slowly enter the house through the open rear doors. There is broken glass all over the floor, the tables and chairs have been thrown about, and there are bullet holes everywhere. The place looks as if a hurricane swept through and then returned for an encore. There are no signs of Nina and no signs of life.

The princess falls to her knees, screaming, "My family, my sons, my Nina, all gone!"

Her hands cover her face as tears chase one another down her cheeks. She looks over to the man God has sent her, a man she has known for such a short period but whom she feels she has known a lifetime.

He walks over and kneels down on the floor next to her and takes her in his arms. She hugs him for comfort and seeks some form of peace. Both are as one with her crying and him trying to comfort her. He places a hand on the side of her head as she slowly reaches up and pulls him down to her waiting lips.

"The ocean is so beautiful," the princess says. "Nina loved to watch the ocean, and the boys loved to play in the water when they were young."

The two sit in the middle of the floor, he wrapped in her and she wrapped in him, as they look out the back of the house at the ocean. The full moon dances upon the sparkling waves; the waves sing as they crash upon the beach; the wind moves gently. It is a calming wind; the explosions have all but stopped.

Kenneth glances across the yard from left to right. "There," he says.

"What, my friend?" she says as her grip on him tightens.

"There at the end of the yard, to the right. There are two wooden doors, like that of a cellar, there are not any locks on the outside," he says as he points toward the far back side of the yard. "Do you know what the doors lead to?"

The princess glances toward the two doors. "No, I assume they are just doors on a storage room."

He jumps to his feet and lifts her straight up. Her arm is over his shoulder, and his arm is around her waist. Their faces are just inches apart. He stops and moves away.

"Please stay here, Princess," he says as he releases her and starts moving to the outside of the house. He runs to the doors, looking in every direction for any Colombian soldiers. There are no sounds, no gunfire, and no explosions.

He slowly reaches down to the wooden doors and tries to open one with a sturdy pull. Nothing happens.

"It's locked from within," he whispers to himself.

He leans down to the doors and says, "Nina, this is Kenneth Douglas. Nina, I know you are in there."

He stands back. Nothing. Once again he leans forward, cupping his mouth with both hands.

"Nina, this is Kenneth Douglas. I have Princess Maria here with me. Please open the doors."

Nothing happens; there is no movement and no sound.

"Nina, please, this is Kenneth Douglas."

Then, a faint sound comes from within the cavern. It's the sound of a locked bolt sliding open.

Then, a small, frightened voice says, "We are here; we are coming out."

Kenneth reaches for one of the doors. The moonlight chases the darkness from below, lighting the path for Nina, Roberto, and Alfonso. The princess watches from the house and sees the three of them exit their underground hiding place. She runs as fast as she can, her arms outstretched toward her sons. Tears flow down her face; her voice cries for her family.

"My family, my sons, my Nina, you are alive. Praise God. Praise Kenneth Douglas," she says as she hugs her sons and Nina.

All four are engulfed in tears of joy, and a smile crosses the face of Kenneth. Once again he feels that strange feeling, that nervous feeling, coming upon him again, that feeling he has not known in so many years—happiness.

Kenneth stands back and watches the reunion. He hears a faint sound of a rifle bolt sliding, as if a bullet was loaded into a chamber. He quickly looks to his left and sees two Colombian soldiers aiming their rifles at the princess.

Kenneth jumps to the princess, placing his chest to her back, his hands upon her shoulders, his face buried into her coal-black hair as two gunshots ring out from the rifles.

The princess feels Kenneth place his hands on her shoulders, feels his breath upon her neck, feels happiness and comfort and security— feels love.

Yes, God, she says to herself, *yes to this man; yes to Kenneth Douglas.*

She feels the warmth of his body against hers.

Suddenly his hands tighten on her shoulders as his head jerks back and his knees buckle; his legs collapse from under his body as the hot lead from the bullets pierce his back.

Kenneth slowly drops to his knees and falls to the ground, looking up to his princess, his eyes locked on hers, his hands reaching for hers.

The princess feels him sliding away from her.

"What? What?" she says as she turns. She screams in horror.

Nina, watching this horrible scene unfold in front of her quickly grabs the sons and pulls them to her.

The princess falls to her knees.

More gunfire sounds, and the two Colombian soldiers drop down dead.

"My princess," a familiar voice says as the princess lies across Kenneth's chest, kissing his lips, but there is no movement from him.

"Please, God, no. Please, God, not again," she cries as she looks up toward heaven.

Captain Eduardo and his men approach from around the house. "My princess," he exclaims, "we have retaken the city. The battle is over."

"Please, Captain. Please help me, and please help him," she cries, looking up to Captain Eduardo as tears once again race down her cheeks, her heart breaking with every beat.

Captain Eduardo looks down at the man, the crop buyer, the American, the special agent, the Panamanian hero, the man whose life is running from his body.

"Hurry, hurry," the captain shouts to his men, "take this man to the hospital, hurry."

Chapter 45

President Navarro stands with his new American friend atop the balcony of the presidential palace as they look over his capital city.

"Well, Colonel, we are separated from Colombia now, thanks to you and your American soldiers. Tomorrow, November 3, 1903, we will be officially separated from Colombian rule. The Republic of Panama has been born, and our hero, Captain Eduardo, the new military commander of Panama, will be honored."

"Yes, Mr. President," Colonel Salvatory says, his head hanging down as a deep sadness covers his face. His voice cracks as he tries to speak. "Many people lost their lives fighting for your country; many good people died that day eleven months ago."

"Ah, Captain Eduardo," the president says as the captain walks out onto the balcony overlooking Panama City. "Tomorrow we honor our separation from Colombian rule and also you, our hero."

The president slaps both hands on the shoulders of his hero.

"Yes, my president," the captain says with a smile across his face.

"Señor President," the captain struggles to get the words out. "There was a man, an American man, who helped us save our country. He established the guerrilla fighters that defeated the Colombian military all across our country and allowed us to win here in Panama City."

The captain and the American advisor stand directly in front of the president. Captain Eduardo softly says, "He saved the princess and your grandsons, Señor President."

"Yes, Captain" the president says as he turns away from both men, his hands clinching tightly to the balcony, his head dropping down, his eyes focused on the palace garden.

"This American, this Kenneth Douglas that you speak of. My daughter never left his side at the hospital. She prayed to God every day to save her friend."

The president turns slowly back to face the men. A small tear escapes his left eye. "I watched her hold his hand for days and brush his hair from his face. She kissed his lips and laid her head across his chest. I watched her cry every day and every night for him to return."

The three men stand together in silence.

"Come, Captain, and you also, Colonel," the president commands of both men as he walks back into the palace. "Let's walk to the ocean. I need to see my daughter."

The three men walk through the palace and out onto the front lawn, followed closely by palace guards.

The president walks toward the palace retreat located several blocks west of the presidential palace. It is a small house of humble design overlooking the ocean from atop the mountains. Captain Eduardo and Colonel Salvatory follow close behind.

The president walks quickly up the front steps, enters the house, and then continues straight through the main family area and out onto the patio that overlooks the ocean below.

"There, Captain" the president says as he points down the hillside to where a couple sits on the ground, looking out over the ocean.

The captain and the American advisor stand next to the president, their eyes searching the hillside below. Suddenly the captain sees Princess Maria and a man sitting next to her, snuggled together and watching the waves as they crash onto the beach below them.

"Kenneth Douglas!" the captain shouts with joy. "But he is dead," the captain says, looking to the president.

The president stands there with a proud look about himself. "No, captain, Kenneth Douglas survived the assault on my daughter. But we must let the Spanish and Colombians believe that he is dead, for he has defeated them in Cuba and now here in Panama."

The president looks over to Colonel Salvatory. "He is with Panama now, my friend. I asked him how Panama could ever repay him for what he has done for us. He told me that God has already taken care of that. His love for Maria and her love for him is all that he asks of this life. They have not been apart since that day."

The three men stand side by side with their hands on the railing of the patio. A sense of euphoria surrounds them as they watch the ocean and the couple below.

The president leans over and says to the American advisor so that the captain cannot hear, "My friend, when Kenneth Douglas was in the hospital those first few months and we did not know if he would survive, he kept mumbling a name: El Diablo Blanco. Do you know what this could possibly mean, Colonel? Do you know who this person is?"

Colonel Salvatory's hands tighten on the railing as a cold, blank stare fills his eyes. His face turns pale, and beads of sweat break out on his forehead.

Princess Maria looks up at the man God sent her and places her head on his shoulder while he reaches down and wraps his arm around her and pulls her to him, holding her ever so close.

Epilogue

I will be walking over to Pach's as soon as I finish this last page. Many of you have asked why we meet on Tuesdays; well, Trish (yes, I married Patricia) is involved in that women's suffrage movement. Ever since the Bull Moose / Republican Party of Teddy's adopted the woman suffrage plank, well, every Tuesday she and several other ladies hold a meeting at the Plant Hotel. The rest of us guys head over to Pach's because we can always count on Cathy for a good home-cooked meal.

My fellow Rough Riders and I appreciate all of the attention that we have received. We do not look upon ourselves as heroes, just ordinary men who answered a call for help from a people who have since extended the hand of friendship.

My thoughts often wonder about the man that I hold so much respect for. Where is he? What great adventure has he been sent on? Greatness and heroism are not something that you are born with, but they are crowns that are placed upon you by someone else for some deed that destiny has cast upon you. Kenneth Douglas never sought the recognition that we thrust upon him, and from what I have seen, from what I heard, he is a man who did not care for or want that attention.

Men like him come along once in a lifetime. They are the people who formed this great nation of ours and who keep us safe from whatever harm may come our way. You can call him Rough Rider, Panamanian/ American hero, Lone Ranger, The Guardian, whatever you choose; I call him my friend.

Charles Santana, Rough Rider
First United States Volunteer Cavalry Regiment